SOCCER IN SUN AND SHADOW

EDUARDO GALEANO

TRANSLATED BY MARK FRIED

VERSO

London • New York

First published by Verso 1998
Paperback edition first published by Verso 1999
Second paperback edition first published by Verso 2003
©Eduardo Galeano 1998, 1999, 2003
Translation © Mark Fried 1998, 1999, 2003

VERSO
UK: 6 Meard Street, London W1F 0EG
USA: 180 Varick Street, New York, NY 10014-4608

Verso is the imprint of New Left Books

Design by POLLEN/Stewart Cauley
Composed in Monotype Bell, Bell Gothic, and Swifty Dingbats
Printed and bound in the USA by Quebecor World Fairfield

ISBN 1-85984-423-5

British Library Cataloguing in Publication Data
A catalogue record for this book is available from the British Library

Library of Congress Cataloging-in-Publication Data
A catalog record for this book is available from the Library of Congress

SOCCER IN SUN AND SHADOW

contents

acknowledgments

This book owes much to the enthusiasm and patience of "El Pepe" Barrientos, "Manolo" Epelbaum, Ezequiel Fernández-Moores, Karl Hubener, Franklin Morales, Angel Ruocco, and Klaus Schuster, all of whom read the drafts, caught mistakes and came up with valuable ideas and information.

Also of great assistance were the critical eye of my wife, Helena Villagra, and the soccer memory of my father, "El Baby" Hughes. My son Claudio and a few friends, or friends of my friends, did their part bringing me books and newspapers or answering queries: Hugo Alfaro, "Zé" Fernando Balbi, Chico Buarque, Nicolás Buenaventura Vidal, Manuel Cabieses, Jorge Consuegra, Pierre Charasse, Julián García-Candau, José González Ortega, "Pancho" Graells, Jens Lohmann, Daniel López D'Alessandro, Sixto Martínez, Juan Manuel Martín Medem, Gianni Miná, Dámaso Murúa, Felipe Nepomuceno, "El Migue" Nieto-Solís, Luis Niño, Luis Ocampos Alonso, Carlos Ossa, Norberto Pérez, Silvia Peyrou, Miguel Angel Ramírez, Alastair Reid, Affonso Romano de Sant'Anna, Rosa Salgado, Giuseppe Smorto and Jorge Valdano. Osvaldo Soriano contributed as guest writer.

I ought to say that all of them are innocent of the result, but the truth is I think they're rather guilty for getting themselves into this mess.

The pages that follow
are dedicated to the children
who once upon a time, years ago,
crossed my path on the Calella de la Costa.
They had been playing soccer and were singing:

We lost, we won,
either way we had fun.

author's confession

LIKE ALL Uruguayan children, I wanted to be a soccer player. I played quite well, in fact I was terrific, but only at night when I was asleep. During the day I was the worst wooden leg ever to set foot on the little soccer fields of my country.

As a fan I also left a lot to be desired. Juan Alberto Schiaffino and Julio César Abbadie played for Peñarol, the enemy team. I was a loyal Nacional fan and I did everything I could to hate them. But with his masterful passes "El Pepe" Schiaffino orchestrated the team's plays as if he were watching from the highest tower of the stadium, and "El Pardo" Abbadie, running in his seven-league boots, would slide the ball all the way down the white touchline, swaying back and forth without ever grazing the ball or his opponents. I couldn't help admiring them, and I even felt like cheering.

Years have gone by and I've finally learned to accept myself for who I am: a beggar for good soccer. I go about the world, hand outstretched, and in the stadiums I plead: "A pretty move, for the love of God."

And when good soccer happens, I give thanks for the miracle and I don't give a damn which team or country performs it.

soccer

THE HISTORY of soccer is a sad voyage from beauty to duty. When the sport became an industry, the beauty that blossoms from the joy of play got torn out by its very roots. In this *fin-de-siècle* world, professional soccer condemns all that is useless, and useless means not profitable. Nobody earns a thing from that crazy feeling that for a moment turns a man into a child playing with a balloon, like a cat with a ball of yarn; a ballet dancer who romps with a ball as light as a balloon or a ball of yarn, playing without even knowing he's playing, with no purpose or clock or referee.

Play has become spectacle, with few protagonists and many spectators, soccer for watching. And that spectacle has become one of the most profitable businesses in the world, organized not for play but rather to impede it. The technocracy of professional sport has managed to impose a soccer of lightning speed and brute strength, a soccer that negates joy, kills fantasy and outlaws daring.

Luckily, on the field you can still see, even if only once in a long while, some insolent rascal who sets aside the script and commits the blunder of dribbling past the entire opposing side, the referee and the crowd in the stands, all for the carnal delight of embracing the forbidden adventure of freedom.

the player

PANTING, he runs up the wing. On one side await the heavens of glory; on the other, ruin's abyss.

He's the envy of the neighborhood: the professional athlete who escaped the factory or the office and gets paid to have fun. He won the lottery. And even if he does have to sweat buckets, with no right to fatigue or failure, he gets into the papers and on TV, his name is on the radio, women swoon over him and children yearn to be like him. But he started out playing for pleasure in the dirt streets of the slums, and now he plays out of duty in stadiums where he has no choice but to win or to win.

Businessmen buy him, sell him, lend him; and he lets it all happen in return for the promise of more fame and more money. The more successful he is and the more money he makes, the more of a prisoner he becomes. Forced to live by military discipline, he suffers the punishing daily round of training and the bombardments of painkillers and cortisone to forget his aches and fool his body. And on the eve of big games, they lock him up in a concentration camp where he does forced labor, eats tasteless food, gets drunk on water and sleeps alone.

In other human trades, decline comes with old age, but a soccer player can be old at thirty. Muscles tire early: "That guy couldn't score if the field were on a slope."

"Him? Not even if they tied the goalie's hands."

Or before thirty if the ball knocks him out badly, or bad luck tears a muscle, or a kick breaks a bone so it can't be fixed. And one rotten day the player discovers he has bet his life on a single card and his money is gone and so is his fame. Fame, that fleeting lady, didn't even leave him a Dear John letter.

the goalkeeper

THEY ALSO call him doorman, keeper, goalie, bouncer or net-minder, but he could just as well be called martyr, pay-all, penitent or punching bag. They say where he walks, the grass never grows.

He's alone, condemned to watch the game from afar. Never leaving the goal, his only company the three posts, he awaits his own execution by firing squad. He used to dress in black, like the referee. Now the referee doesn't have to dress like a crow and the goalkeeper can populate his solitude with colorful fantasies.

He doesn't score goals, he's there to keep them from being scored. The goal is soccer's fiesta: the striker sparks delight and the goalkeeper, a wet blanket, snuffs it out.

He wears the number one on his back. The first to be pai? No, the first to pay. It's always the keeper's fault. And if it isn't, he still gets blamed. When any player commits a foul, he's the one who gets punished: they leave him there in the

immensity of the empty net, abandoned to face his executioner alone. And when the team has a bad afternoon, he's the one
who pays the bill, expiating the sins of others under a rain of
flying balls.

The rest of the players can blow it once in a while, or
often, then redeem themselves with a spectacular dribble, a
masterful pass, a well-placed volley. Not him. The crowd
never forgives the keeper. Was he drawn out by a fake? Left
looking ridiculous? Did the ball skid? Did his fingers of steel
turn to silk? With a single slip-up the goalie can ruin a game
or lose a championship, and the fans suddenly forget all his
feats and condemn him to eternal disgrace. Damnation will
follow him to the end of his days.

the idol

AND ONE fine day the goddess of the wind kisses the foot of
man, that mistreated, scorned foot, and from that kiss the soccer idol is born. He is born in a straw crib in a tin-roofed
shack and he enters the world clinging to a ball.

From the moment he learns to walk, he knows how to play.
In his early years he brings joy to the sandlots, plays like crazy in
the back alleys of the slums until night falls and you can't see the
ball, and in his early manhood he takes flight and the stadiums

fly with him. His acrobatic art draws multitudes, Sunday after Sunday, from victory to victory, ovation to ovation.

The ball seeks him out, knows him, needs him. She rests and rocks on the top of his foot. He caresses her and makes her speak, and in that tête-a-tête millions of mutes converse. The nobodies, those condemned to always be nobodies, feel they are somebodies for a moment by virtue of those one-two passes, those dribbles that draw Z's on the grass, those incredible backheel goals or overhead volleys. When he plays, the team has twelve players: "Twelve? It has fifteen! Twenty!"

The ball laughs, radiant, in the air. He brings her down, puts her to sleep, showers her with compliments, dances with her, and seeing such things never before seen his admirers pity their unborn grandchildren who will never see them.

But the idol is an idol for only a moment, a human eterni-ty, all of nothing; and when the time comes for the golden foot to become a lame duck, the star will have completed his jour-ney from sparkle to blackout. His body has more patches than a clown's suit, and by now the acrobat is a cripple, the artist a beast of burden: "Not with your clodhoppers!"

The fountain of public adulation becomes the lightning rod of public rancor: "You mummy!"

Sometimes the idol doesn't fall all at once. And some-times when he breaks, people devour the pieces.

the fan

ONCE A WEEK, the fan flees his house and goes to the stadium.

Banners wave and the air resounds with noisemakers, firecrackers and drums, it rains streamers and confetti. The city disappears, its routine forgotten, all that exists is the temple. In this sacred place, the only religion without atheists puts its divinities on display. Although the fan can contemplate the miracle more comfortably on TV, he prefers to make the pilgrimage to this spot where he can see his angels in the flesh doing battle with the demons of the day.

Here the fan shakes his handkerchief, gulps his saliva, swallows his bile, eats his cap, whispers prayers and curses and suddenly breaks out in an ovation, leaping like a flea to hug the stranger at his side cheering the goal. While the pagan mass lasts, the fan is many. Along with thousands of other devotees he shares the certainty that we are the best, that all referees are crooked, that all the adversaries cheat.

Rarely does the fan say: "My club plays today." Rather he says: "We play today." He knows it's "player number twelve" who stirs up the winds of fervor that propel the ball when she falls asleep, just as the other eleven players know that playing without their fans is like dancing without music.

When the game is over, the fan, who has not moved from the stands, celebrates *his* victory: "What a goal we scored," "What a beating we gave them." Or he cries over *his* defeat: "They swindled us again," "Thief of a referee." And then the sun goes down and so does the fan. Shadows fall over the emptying stadium. On the concrete terracing, a few fleeting bonfires burn, while the lights and voices fade. The stadium is left alone and the fan, too, returns to his solitude: to the I who had been we. The fan goes off, the crowd breaks up and melts away, and Sunday becomes as melancholy as Ash Wednesday after the death of carnival.

the fanatic

THE FANATIC is a fan in a madhouse. His mania for denying all evidence finally upended whatever once passed for his mind, and the remains of the shipwreck spin about aimlessly in waters whipped by a fury that gives no quarter.

The fanatic shows up at the stadium wrapped in the team flag, his face painted the colors of their beloved shirts, prickling with strident and aggressive paraphernalia, and on the way he makes a lot of noise and a lot of fuss. He never comes alone. In the midst of the rowdy crowd, dangerous centipede, this cowed man will cow others, this frightened man becomes frightening. Omnipotence on Sunday exorcises the obedient life he leads the rest of the week: the bed with no desire, the job with no calling or no job at all. Liberated for a day, the fanatic has much to avenge.

In an epileptic fit he watches the game but doesn't see it. His arena is the stands. They are his battleground. The mere presence of a fan of the other side constitutes an inexcusable provocation. Good isn't violent by nature, but Evil leaves it no choice. The enemy, always in the wrong, deserves a good thrashing. The fanatic cannot let his mind wander because the enemy is everywhere, even in that quiet spectator who at any moment might offer the opinion that the rival team is playing fair; then he'll get what he deserves.

the goal

THE GOAL is soccer's orgasm. And like orgasms, goals have become an ever less frequent occurrence in modern life.

Half a century ago, it was a rare thing for a game to end scoreless: 0–0, two open mouths, two yawns. Now, the eleven players spend the entire game hanging from the crossbars, trying to stop goals, and have no time to score them.

The excitement unleashed whenever the white bullet makes the net ripple might appear mysterious or crazy, but remember the miracle doesn't happen very often. The goal, even if it be a little one, is always a gooooooooooooooooooooooooal in the throat of the commentators, a "do" sung from the chest that would leave Caruso forever mute, and the crowd goes nuts and the stadium forgets that it's made of concrete and breaks free of the earth and flies through the air.

the referee

IN SPANISH he's the *árbitro* and he's arbitrary by definition. An abominable tyrant who runs his dictatorship without opposition, a pompous executioner who exercises his absolute power with an operatic flourish. Whistle between his lips, he blows the winds of inexorable fate either to allow a goal or to disallow one. Card in hand, he raises the colors of doom: yellow to punish the sinner and oblige him to repent, and red to force him into exile.

The linesmen, who assist but do not rule, look on from the side. Only the referee steps onto the playing field, and he's absolutely right to cross himself when he first appears before the roaring crowd. His job is to make himself hated. The only universal sentiment in soccer: everybody hates him. He always gets catcalls, never applause.

No one runs more. The only one obliged to run the entire game without pause, this interloper who pants in the ears of every player breaks his back galloping like a horse. And in return for his pains, the crowd howls for his head. From beginning to end he sweats oceans, forced to chase the white ball that skips along back and forth between the feet of everyone else. Of course he'd love to play, but never has he been offered that privilege. When the ball hits him by accident, the entire stadium curses his mother. But even so, just to be there in that sacred green space where the ball floats and glides, he's willing to suffer insults, catcalls, stones and damnation.

Sometimes, though rarely, his judgment coincides with the inclinations of the fans, but not even then does he emerge unscathed. The losers owe their loss to him and the winners triumph in spite of him. Scapegoat for every error, cause of every misfortune, the fans would have to invent him if he didn't already exist. The more they hate him, the more they need him.

For over a century the referee dressed in mourning. For whom? For himself. Now he wears bright colors to mask his feelings.

the manager

IN THE OLD days there was the trainer and nobody paid him much heed. He died without a word when the game stopped being a game and professional soccer required a technocracy to keep people in line. Then the manager was born. His mission: to prevent improvisation, restrict freedom and maximize the productivity of the players, who were now obliged to become disciplined athletes.

The trainer used to say: "Let's play."

The manager says: "Let's go to work."

Today they talk in numbers. The history of soccer in the twentieth century, a journey from daring to fear, is a trip from the 2-3-5 to the 5-4-1 by way of the 4-3-3 and the 4-4-2. Any ignoramus could translate that much with a little help, but the rest is impossible. The manager dreams up formulas as mysterious as the Immaculate Conception, and he uses them to develop tactical schemes more indecipherable than the Holy Trinity.

From the old blackboard to the electronic screen: now great plays are planned by computer and taught by video. These dream-manoeuvers are rarely seen in the broadcast version of the games. Television prefers to focus on the furrows in the manager's brow. We see him gnawing his fists or shouting instructions that would certainly turn the game around if anyone could understand them.

Journalists pepper him with questions at the post-game press conference, but he never reveals the secrets of his victories, although he formulates admirable explanations of his defeats. "The instructions were clear, but they didn't listen," he says when the team suffers a big defeat to a crummy rival. Or he talks about himself in the third person to dispel any doubts, more or less like this: "The reverses the team suffered today will never mar the achievement of a conceptual clarity that this manager once described as a synthesis of the many sacrifices required to become truly effective."

The machinery of spectacle grinds up everything in its path, nothing lasts very long, and the manager is as disposable as any other product of consumer society. Today the crowd screams, "Never die!" and next Sunday they invite him to kill himself.

The manager believes soccer is a science and the field a laboratory, but the genius of Einstein and the subtlety of Freud isn't enough for the owners and the fans. They want a miracleworker like the Virgin of Lourdes, with the stamina of Gandhi.

the theater

THE PLAYERS in this show act with their legs for an audience of thousands or millions who watch from the stands or their living rooms with their souls on edge. Who writes the play—the manager? This play mocks its author, unfolding as it pleases and according to the actors' abilities. It definitely depends on fate, which like the wind blows every which way. That's why the outcome is always a surprise to spectators and protagonists alike, except in cases of bribery or other inescapable tricks of destiny.

How many small theaters inhabit the great theater of soccer? How many stages fit inside that rectangle of green grass? Not all players act with their legs alone. Some are masterful actors in the art of tormenting their fellow players. Wearing the mask of a saint incapable of harming a fly, such a man will spit at his opponent, insult him, push him, throw dirt in his eyes, give him a well-placed elbow to the chin, dig another into his ribs, pull his hair or his shirt, step on his foot when he stops or his hand when he's down—and all behind the referee's back, while the linesman contemplates the passing clouds.

Some are wizards in the art of gaining advantage. Wearing the mask of a poor sad-sack who looks like an imbecile but is really an idiot, such a player will take a penalty, a free kick or a throw-in several leagues beyond the point indicated by the referee. And when he has to form a wall, he glides over to the spot very slowly, without lifting his feet, until the magic carpet deposits him right on top of the player about to kick the ball.

There are actors unsurpassed in the art of wasting time. Wearing the mask of a recently crucified martyr, such a player rolls in agony, clutching his knee or his head, and then lies prone on the grass. Minutes pass. At a snail's pace out comes the fat masseur, the holy-hand, running with sweat, smelling of liniment, wearing a towel around his neck and carrying a flask in one hand and some infallible potion in the other. Hours go by, years go by, until the referee orders them to take that corpse off the field. Suddenly, up jumps the player, whoosh, and the miracle of resurrection occurs.

the specialists

BEFORE THE GAME, the reporters formulate their disconcerting question: "Are you ready to win?"

And they obtain an astonishing answer: "We will do everything possible to obtain victory."

Later, the broadcasters take the floor. TV anchors just keep the images company, they know they can't compete. Radio commentators, on the other hand, are a less faint-hearted breed. These masters of suspense do more running than the players and more skidding than the ball itself. With dizzying speed they describe a game that bears little resemblance to the one you're watching. In that waterfall of words the shot you see scraping the sky is actually grazing the crossbar, and the net where a spider placidly spins her web from post to post while the goalkeeper yawns is facing an imminent goal.

When the vibrant day is over in the concrete colossus, it is the critics' turn. Already they have interrupted the broadcast several times to tell the players what to do, but the players didn't listen because they were too busy making mistakes. These ideologues of the WM formation against the MW, which is the same thing but backwards, use a language where scientific erudition alternates with war propaganda and lyrical ecstasy. And they always speak in the plural, because they are many.

the language of soccer doctors

LET'S SUM UP our point of view, formulating a first approximation of the tactical, technical and physical problems of the contest waged this afternoon on the field of the Unidos Venceremos Soccer Club without turning to simplifications incompatible with this topic, which without a doubt demands a more profound and detailed analysis, and without resorting to ambiguities which have been, are and always will be alien to our lifelong dedication to serving the sporting public.

It would be easy for us to evade our responsibility and attribute the home team's setback to the restrained performance of its players, but the excessive sluggishness they undeniably demonstrated in today's game each time they received the ball in no way justifies, understand me well ladies and gentlemen, *in no way* justifies such a generalized and therefore unjust critique. No, no, and no. Conformity is not our style, as those of you who have followed us during the long years of our career well know, not only in our beloved country but on the stages of international and even worldwide sport, wherever we have been called upon to fulfill our humble duty. So, as is our custom, we are going to pronounce all the syllables of every word: the organic potential of the game-plan pursued by this struggling team has not been crowned with success simply and plainly because the team continues to be incapable of adequately channelling its expectations for greater offensive projection in the direction of the enemy goal. We said as much only this past Sunday and we affirm it today, with our head held high and without any hairs on our tongue, because we have always called a spade a spade and we will continue speaking the truth, though it hurts, fall who may, and no matter the cost.

choreographed war

IN SOCCER, ritual sublimation of war, eleven men in shorts are the sword of the neighborhood, the city or the nation. These warriors without weapons or armor exorcize the demons of the crowd and reaffirm its faith: in each confrontation between two sides, old hatreds and old loves passed from father to son enter into combat.

The stadium has towers and banners like a castle, as well as a deep and wide moat around the field. In the middle, a white line separates the territories in dispute. At each end stand the goals to be bombed with flying balls. The area directly in front of the goals is called the "danger zone."

In the center circle, the captains exchange pennants and shake hands as the ritual demands. The referee blows his whistle and the ball, another whistling wind, is set in motion. The ball travels back and forth, a player traps her and takes her for a ride until he's pummeled in a tackle and falls spread-eagled. The victim does not rise. In the immensity of the green expanse, the player lies prostrate. From the immensity of the stands, voices thunder. The enemy crowd emits a friendly roar:

"*¡Que se muera!*"
"*Devi morire!*"
"*Tuez-le!*"
"*Mach ihn nieder!*"
"*Let him die!*"
"*Kill kill kill!*"

the language of war

UTILIZING A competent tactical variant of their planned strategy, our squad leapt to the charge, surprising the enemy unprepared. It was a brutal attack. When the home troops invaded enemy territory, our battering ram opened a breach in the most vulnerable flank of the defensive wall and infiltrated the danger zone. The artillery man received the projectile and with a skillful manoeuvre he got into shooting position, reared back for the kill and brought the attack to culmination with a cannonball that annihilated the guard. Then the defeated sentry, custodian of the bastion that had appeared unassailable, fell to his knees with his face in his hands while the executioner who shot him raised his arms to the cheering crowd.

The enemy did not retreat, but its stampedes never managed to sow panic in the home trenches, and time and again they crashed against our well-armored rearguard. Their men were shooting with wet powder, reduced to impotence by the gallantry of our gladiators, who battled like lions. When two of ours were knocked out of the fight, the crowd called in vain for the maximum sentence, but such atrocities fit for war and disrespectful of the gentlemanly rules of the noble sport of soccer continued with impunity.

At last, when the deaf and blind referee called an end to the contest, a well-deserved whistle discharged the defeated squad. Then the victorious people invaded the redoubt to hoist on their shoulders the eleven heroes of this epic gest, this grand feat, this great exploit that cost us so much blood, sweat and tears. And our captain, wrapped in the standard of our fatherland that will never again be soiled by defeat, raised up the trophy and kissed the great silver cup. It was the kiss of glory!

the stadium

HAVE YOU ever entered an empty stadium? Try it. Stand in the middle of the field and listen. There is nothing less empty than an empty stadium. There is nothing less mute than the stands bereft of people.

At Wembley, shouts from the '66 World Cup which England won still resound, and if you listen very closely you can hear groans from 1953 when England fell to the Hungarians. Montevideo's Centenario Stadium sighs with nostalgia for the glory days of Uruguayan soccer. Maracaná is still crying over Brazil's 1950 World Cup defeat. At Bombonera in Buenos Aires, drums boom from half a century ago. From the depths of Azteca Stadium, you can hear the ceremonial chants of the ancient Mexican ball game. The concrete terraces of Camp Nou in Barcelona speak Catalán, and the stands of San Mamés in Bilbao talk in Euskera. In Milan, the ghost of Giuseppe Meazza scores goals that shake the stadium bearing his name. The final of the '74 World Cup, won by Germany, is played day after day and night after night at Munich's Olympic Stadium. The stadium of King Fahad in Saudi Arabia has marble and gold boxes and carpeted stands, but it has no memory or much of anything to say.

the ball

THE CHINESE used a ball made of leather and filled with hemp. In the time of the Pharaohs the Egyptians used a ball made of straw or the husks of seeds, wrapped in colorful cloths. The Greeks and Romans used an ox bladder, inflated and sewn shut. Europeans of the Middle Ages and the Renaissance played with an oval-shaped ball filled with horsehair. In America the ball was made of rubber and bounced like nowhere else. The chroniclers of the Spanish court tell how Hernán Cortés bounced a Mexican ball high in the air before the bulging eyes of Emperor Charles.

The rubber chamber, swollen with air and covered with leather, was born in the middle of the last century thanks to the genius of Charles Goodyear, an American from Connecticut. And long after that, thanks to the genius of Tossolini, Valbonesi and Polo, three Argentines from Córdoba, the lace-free ball was born. They invented a chamber with a valve inflated by injection, and ever since the 1938 World Cup it has been possible to

head the ball without getting hurt by the laces that used to tie
it together.

Until the middle of this century, the ball was brown. Then
white. In our days it comes in different patterns of black on a
white background. Now it has a waist of sixty centimeters and
is dressed in polyurethane on polyethylene foam. Waterproof,
it weighs less than half a kilo and travels more quickly than the
old leather ball, which on rainy days barely moved.

They call it by many names: the sphere, the round, the
tool, the globe, the balloon, the projectile. In Brazil no one
doubts the ball is a woman. Brazilians call her pudgy, *gorduch-
inha*, or baby, *menina*, and they give her names like Maricota,
Leonor or Margarita.

Pelé kissed her in Maracaná when he scored his thousandth goal and Di Stéfano built her a monument in front of
his house, a bronze ball with a plaque that says: *Thanks, old girl.*

She is loyal. In the final game of the 1930 World Cup, both
teams insisted on playing with their own ball. Sage as Solomon,
the referee decided that the first half would be played with the
Argentine ball and the second with the Uruguayan ball.
Argentina won the first half, and Uruguay the second. The
ball can also be fickle sometimes, refusing to enter the goal
because she changes her mind in midflight and curves away.
You see, she is easily offended. She can't stand getting kicked
around or hit out of spite. She insists on being caressed, kissed,
lulled to sleep on the chest or the foot. She is proud, vain perhaps, and she's not lacking a motive: she knows all too well that
when she rises gracefully she brings joy to many hearts, and
many a heart is crushed when she lands without style.

the origins

IN SOCCER, as in almost everything else, the Chinese were first. Five thousand years ago, Chinese jugglers had balls dancing on their feet, and it wasn't long before they organized the first games. The net was in the center of the field and the players had to keep the ball from touching the ground without using their hands. The sport continued from dynasty to dynasty, as can be seen on certain bas-relief monuments from long before Christ, and in later Ming Dynasty engravings which show people playing with a ball that could have been made by Adidas.

We know that in ancient times the Egyptians and the Japanese had fun kicking a ball around. On the marble surface of a Greek tomb from five centuries before Christ a man is kneeing a ball. The comedies of Antiphanes contain telling expressions like *long ball, short pass, forward pass*. . . . They say that Emperor Julius Caesar was quick with his feet, and that Nero couldn't score at all. In any case, there is no doubt that while Jesus lay dying on the cross the Romans were playing something fairly similar to soccer.

Roman legionaries kicked the ball all the way to the British Isles. Centuries later, in 1314, King Edward II stamped his seal on a royal decree condemning the game as plebeian and riotous: "Forasmuch as there is a great noise in the city caused by hustling over large balls, from which many evils may arise, which God forbid." Football, as it was already being called, left a slew of victims. Matches were fought by gangs, and there were no limits on the number of players, the length of the game or anything else. An entire town would play against another town, advancing with kicks and punches toward the goal, which at that time was a far-off windmill. The games extended over several leagues and several days at the cost of several lives. Kings repeatedly outlawed these bloody events: in 1349, Edward III included soccer among games that were "stupid and utterly useless," and there were edicts against the game signed by Henry IV in 1410 and Henry VI in 1447. These only confirmed that prohibition whets the appetite, because the more it was banned, the more it was played.

In 1592 in *The Comedy of Errors*, Shakespeare turned to soccer to formulate a character's complaint: "Am I so round with you as you with me, / that like a football you do spurn me thus? / You spurn me hence, and he will spurn me hither. / If I last in this service you must case me in leather." And a few years later in *King Lear*, the Earl of Kent taunted: "Nor tripped neither, you base football player!"

In Florence soccer was called *calcio* as it still is throughout Italy. Leonardo da Vinci was a fervent fan and Machiavelli loved to play. It was played in sides of twenty-seven men split into three lines, and they were allowed to use their hands and feet to hit the ball and gouge the bellies of their adversaries. Throngs of people attended the matches, which were held in the largest plazas and on the frozen waters of the Arno. Far from Florence, in the gardens of the Vatican, Popes Clement VII, Leo IX and Urban VIII used to roll up their vestments to play *calcio*.

In Mexico and Central America a rubber ball filled in for the sun in a sacred ceremony performed as far back as 1500 BC.

But we don't know when soccer began in many parts of the Americas. The Indians of the Bolivian Amazon say they have been kicking a hefty rubber ball between two posts since time immemorial. In the eighteenth century, a Spanish priest from the Jesuit missions of the Upper Paraná described an ancient custom of the Guaraníes: "They do not throw the ball with their hands like us, rather they propel it with the upper part of their bare foot." Among the Indians of Mexico and Central America, the ball was generally hit with the hip or the forearm, although paintings at Teotihuacán and Chichén-Itzá show the ball being kicked with the foot and the knee. A mural created over a thousand years ago in Tepantitla has a grandfather of Hugo Sánchez manoeuvering the ball with his left. The game would end when the ball approached its destination: the sun arrived at dawn after travelling through the region of death. Then, for the sun to rise, blood would flow. According to some in the know, the Aztecs had the habit of sacrificing the winners. Before cutting off their heads, they painted red stripes on their bodies. The chosen of the gods would offer their blood, so the earth would be fertile and the heavens generous.

the rules of the game

AFTER SO MANY centuries of official denial, the British Isles finally accepted the ball in its destiny. Under Queen Victoria soccer was embraced not only as a plebeian vice, but as an aristocratic virtue.

The future leaders of society learned how to win by playing soccer in the courtyards of colleges and universities. There, upper-class pups unbosomed their youthful ardors, honed their discipline, tempered their anger and sharpened their wits. At the other end of the social scale, the workers had no need to test the limits of their bodies, since that's what factories and workshops were for, but the fatherland of industrial capitalism discovered that soccer, passion of the masses, offered entertainment and consolation to the poor and distraction from thoughts of strikes and other evils.

In its modern form, soccer comes from a gentleman's agreement signed by twelve English clubs in the autumn of 1863 in a London tavern. The clubs agreed to abide by rules established in 1846 by the University of Cambridge. At Cambridge soccer divorced rugby: carrying the ball with your hands was outlawed, although touching it was allowed, and kicking the adversary was also prohibited. "Kicks must be aimed only at the ball," warned one rule. A century and a half later some players still confuse the ball with their rival's skull, owing to the similarity in shape.

The London accord put no limit on the number of players, or the size of the field, or the height of the goal, or the length of the game. Games lasted two or three hours and the protagonists chatted and smoked whenever the ball was flying in the distance. One modern rule was established: the off-side. It was disloyal to score goals behind the adversary's back.

In those days no one played a particular position on the field: they all ran happily after the ball, each wherever he wanted, and everyone changed positions at will. It fell to Scotland, in around 1870, to organize teams with defense, midfielders and strikers. By then sides had eleven players. From 1869 on, none of them could touch the ball with their hands, not even to catch and drop it to kick. In 1871 the exception to that taboo was born: the goalkeeper could use his entire body to defend the goal.

The goalkeeper protected a square redoubt narrower than today's and much higher. It consisted of two posts joined by a belt, five and a half meters off the ground. The belt was replaced by a wooden crossbar in 1875. Goals were literally scored on the posts with a small notch. Today goals are registered on electronic scoreboards but the expression "to score a goal" stuck. In some countries we call the goalmouth the *arco*, and the one who defends it the *arquero*, even though it's all right angles and not an arch at all, perhaps because students at English colleges used courtyard arches for goals.

In 1872 the referee made his appearance. Until then the players were their own judges, and they themselves sanctioned any fouls committed. In 1880, chronometer in hand, the referee became the judge of when the game was over and when anyone should be sent off, though he still ran things by shouting from the sidelines. In 1891 the referee stepped onto the playing field for the first time, blowing a whistle to call the first penalty kick in history and walking twelve paces to indicate the spot where it was to be taken. For some time the British press had been campaigning in favor of penalties because the players needed some protection in front of the goal, which was the scene of incredible butchery. A hair-raising list of players killed and bones broken had been published in the *Westminster Gazette.*

In 1882 English authorities allowed the throw-in. Eight years later the areas of the field were marked with lime and a circle was drawn in the center. That same year the goal gained a net to trap the ball and erase any doubts about whether a goal had been scored.

After that the century died, and with it the British monopoly. In 1904, FIFA was born, the Fédération Internationale de Football Associations, which has governed relations between ball and foot throughout the world ever since. Through all the world championships held since, few changes have been made to the British rules which first organized the sport.

the english invasions

OUTSIDE THE MADHOUSE, in an empty lot in Buenos Aires, several blond boys were kicking a ball around.

"Who are they?" asked a child.

"Crazy people," answered his father. "Crazy English."

Journalist Juan José de Soiza Reilly remembers this from his childhood. At first, soccer seemed like a crazy man's game in the River Plate. But with the expansion of the Empire, soccer became an export as typically British as Manchester cloth, railways, loans from Barings or the doctrine of free trade. It arrived on the feet of sailors who played by the dikes of Buenos Aires and Montevideo, while Her Majesty's ships unloaded blankets, boots and flour, and took on wool, hides and wheat to make more blankets, boots and flour on the other side of the world. English citizens, diplomats and managers of railway and gas companies, formed the first local teams. The English of Montevideo and Buenos Aires staged Uruguay's first international competition in 1889, under a gigantic portrait of Queen Victoria, her eyes lowered in a mask of disdain. Another portrait of the queen of the seas watched over the first Brazilian soccer game in 1895, played between the British subjects of the Gas Company and the São Paulo Railway.

Old photographs show these pioneers in sepia tones. They were warriors trained for battle. Cotton and wool armor covered their entire bodies so as not to offend the ladies in attendance, who unfurled silk parasols and waved lace handkerchiefs. The only flesh the players exposed were their serious faces peering out from behind wax-twirled mustaches below caps or hats. Their feet were shod with heavy Mansfield shoes.

It didn't take long to become contagious. Sooner rather than later, the native-born gentlemen of local society started playing that crazy English game. They imported from London the shirts, shoes, thick ankle-socks and shorts which reached from the chest to below the knee. Balls no longer confounded customs officers, who at first hadn't known how to classify the species. Ships also brought rule books to these far-off coasts of southern America, and with them came words which remained for many years to come: *field, score, goal, goalkeeper, back, half, forward, out-ball, penalty, off-side.* A "foul" merited punishment by the "referee," but the aggrieved player could accept an apology from the guilty party "as long as his apology was sincere and was expressed in correct English," according to the first soccer rule book that circulated in the River Plate.

Meanwhile, other English words were being incorporated into the speech of Latin American countries in the Caribbean: *pitcher, catcher, innings.* Having fallen under U.S. influence, these countries learned to hit a ball with a rounded wooden bat. The Marines shouldered bats next to their rifles when they imposed imperial order on the region by blood and fire. Baseball became for the people of the Caribbean what soccer is for us.

creole soccer

THE ARGENTINE football association did not allow Spanish to be spoken at the meetings of its directors, and the Uruguay Association Football League outlawed Sunday games because it was British custom to play on Saturday. But by the first years of the century, soccer was becoming popular and nationalized on the shores of the River Plate. This diversion, first imported to entertain the lazy offspring of the well-off, had escaped from its high window-box, came to earth and was setting down roots.

The process was unstoppable. Like the tango, soccer blossomed in the slums. It required no money and could be played with nothing more than sheer desire. In fields, in alleys and on beaches, native-born kids and young immigrants improvised games using balls made of old socks filled with rags or paper, and a couple of stones for a goal. Thanks to the language of the game, which soon became universal, workers driven out of the countryside could communicate perfectly well with workers driven out of Europe. The Esperanto of the ball connected poor Creoles with peons who had crossed the sea from Vigo, Lisbon, Naples, Beirut or Besarabia with their dreams of *"hacer la América"*—making a new world by building, carrying, baking or sweeping. Soccer had made a lovely voyage: first organized in the colleges and universities of England, it brought joy to the lives of South Americans who had never set foot in a school.

On the fields of Buenos Aires and Montevideo, a style was born. A home-grown way of playing soccer, like the home-grown way of dancing which was being invented in the milonga clubs. Dancers drew filigrees on a single floor tile, and soccer players created their own language in that tiny space where they chose to retain and possess the ball rather than kick it, as if their feet were hands braiding the leather. On the feet of the first Creole *virtuosos el toque*, the touch, was born: the ball was strummed as if it were a guitar, a source of music.

At the same time, soccer was being tropicalized in Rio de Janeiro and São Paulo by the poor who enriched it while they appropriated it. No longer the possession of the few comfortable youths who played by copying, this foreign sport became Brazilian, fertilized by the creative energies of the people discovering it. And thus was born the most beautiful soccer in the world, made of hip feints, undulations of the torso and legs in flight, all of which came from *capoeira*, the warrior dance of black slaves, and from the joyful dances of the big-city slums.

As soccer became a popular passion and revealed its hidden beauty, it disqualified itself as a dignified pastime. In 1915 the democratization of soccer drew complaints from the Rio de Janeiro magazine *Sports*: "Those of us who have a certain position in society are obliged to play with workers, with drivers. . . . The playing of sports is becoming an agony, a sacrifice, never a diversion."

the story of fla and flu

1912 SAW the first classic in the history of Brazilian soccer: the first Fla-Flu. Fluminense beat Flamengo 3-2.

The match was active and violent, causing numerous fainting spells among the spectators. The boxes were festooned with flowers, fruits, feathers, drooping ladies and raucous gentlemen. While the gentlemen celebrated each goal by throwing their straw hats onto the playing field, the ladies let their fans fall and collapsed from the excitement of the goal or the oppression of heat and corset.

Flamengo had been born not long before, when Fluminense split in two after much saber rattling and many labor pains. Soon the father was sorry he hadn't strangled this smart aleck of a son in the crib, but it was too late. Fluminense had spawned its own curse and nothing could be done.

From then on, father and son—rebellious son, abandoned father—dedicated their lives to hating each other. Each Fla-Flu classic is a new battle in a war without end. The two love the same city, lazy, sinful Rio de Janeiro, a city that languidly lets herself be loved, toying with both and surrendering to neither. Father and son play for the lover who plays with them. For her they battle, and she attends each duel dressed for a party.

the opiate of the people?

HOW IS soccer like God? Each inspires devotion among believers and distrust among intellectuals.

In 1902 in London, Rudyard Kipling made fun of soccer and those who contented their souls with "the muddied oafs at the goals." Three-quarters of a century later in Buenos Aires, Jorge Luis Borges was more subtle: he gave a lecture on the subject of immortality on the same day and at the same hour that Argentina was playing its first game in the '78 World Cup.

The scorn of many conservative intellectuals comes from their belief that soccer-worship is exactly the religion people deserve. Possessed by soccer, the proles think with their feet, which is the only way they can think, and through such primitive ecstasy they fulfill their dreams. The animal instinct overtakes human reason, ignorance crushes culture, and the riff-raff get what they want.

In contrast, many leftist intellectuals denigrate soccer because it castrates the masses and derails their revolutionary ardor. Bread and circus, circus without the bread: hypnotized by the ball, which exercises a perverse fascination, workers' consciousness becomes atrophied and they let themselves be led about like sheep by their class enemies.

In the River Plate, once the English and the rich lost possession of the sport, the first popular clubs were organized in railway workshops and shipyards. Several anarchist and socialist leaders soon denounced the clubs as a manoeuver by the bourgeoisie to forestall strikes and disguise class divisions. The spread of soccer throughout the world was an imperialist trick to keep oppressed peoples in an eternal childhood, unable to grow up.

But the club Argentinos Juniors was born with the name Chicago Martyrs, in homage to those anarchist workers, and May First was the day chosen to launch the club Chacarita in a Buenos Aires anarchist library. In those first years of the century, plenty of left-leaning intellectuals celebrated soccer instead of repudiating it as a sedative of consciousness. Among them, the Italian Marxist Antonio Gramsci praised "this open-air kingdom of human loyalty."

a flag that rolls

DURING THE summer of 1916, in the midst of the World War, an English captain named Neville launched a military attack by kicking a ball. He leapt out from behind the parapet that offered him some cover, and chased the ball toward the German trenches. His regiment, at first hesitant, followed. The captain was cut down by gunfire, but England conquered that no-man's-land and celebrated the battle as the first victory of British soccer on the front lines.

Many years later, toward the end of this century, the owner of Milan won the Italian elections with a chant from the stadiums, *"Forza Italia!"* Silvio Berlusconi promised to save Italy the way he had saved Milan's all-time champion superteam, and voters forgot that several of his companies were on the edge of ruin.

Soccer and fatherland are always connected, and politicians and dictators frequently exploit those links of identity. In '34 and '38, the Italian squad won the World Cup in the name of the fatherland and Mussolini, and the players started and finished each game by saluting the crowd with their rights arms outstretched, giving three cheers for Italy.

For the Nazis, too, soccer was a matter of state. A monument in the Ukraine commemorates the players of the 1942 Dynamo Kiev team. During the German occupation they committed the insane act of defeating Hitler's squad in the local stadium. Having been warned, "If you win, you die," they started out resigned to losing, trembling with fear and hunger, but in the end they could not resist the temptation of dignity. When the game was over all eleven were shot with their shirts on at the edge of a cliff.

Soccer and fatherland, fatherland and soccer: in 1934 while Bolivia and Paraguay were annihilating each other in the Chaco War, disputing a deserted corner of the map, the Paraguayan Red Cross formed a team that played in several Argentinian and Uruguayan cities and raised enough money to attend to the wounded of both sides.

Three years later, while General Franco, arm in arm with Hitler and Mussolini, bombed the Spanish Republic, a Basque team was on the road in Europe and Barcelona was playing in the United States and Mexico. The Basque government had

sent the Euzkadi team to France and other countries to pub-
licize their cause and raise funds for defense; Barcelona had
sailed for America with the same mission. It was 1937 and
Barcelona's president had already fallen under Franco's bullets. On the soccer field and off, both teams embodied democracy under siege.

Only four of Barcelona's players made it back to Spain
during the war. Of the Basques, only one. When the Republic
was defeated, FIFA declared the exiled players to be in rebel-
lion and threatened them with permanent suspension, but a
few managed to find positions with Latin American teams.
Several of the Basques formed club España in Mexico who
was unbeatable in its early years. The Euzkadi center forward, Isidro Lángara, made his debut in Argentina in 1939.
In his first match he scored four goals. That was for San
Lorenzo, where Angel Zubieta, who had played in Euzkadi's
midfield, also starred. Later on, in Mexico, Lángara led the
list of scorers in the 1945 championship.

The model club of Franco's Spain, Real Madrid, ruled
the world between 1956 and 1960. This astonishing team
won four cups in a row in the Spanish League, five European
Cups and one Intercontinental. Real Madrid went everywhere and always left people with their mouths open. The
Franco dictatorship had found a travelling embassy that
couldn't be beat. Goals broadcast over the radio were more
effective trumpets of triumph than the anthem "Cara al Sol."
In 1959 one of the regime's political bosses, José Solís, voiced
his gratitude to the players: "Thanks to you, people who used
to hate us now understand us." Like El Cid, Real Madrid

embodied all the virtues of Immortal Spain, but it looked more like the Foreign Legion. This famous squad starred a Frenchman, Kopa, two Argentines, Di Stéfano and Rial, the Uruguayan Santamaría and the Hungarian Puskas.

Ferenc Puskas was called "Little Cannon Boom" for the smashing virtues of his left leg, which was as supple as a fine leather glove. Other Hungarians, Laislao Kubala, Zoltan Czibor and Sandor Kocsis, starred with Barcelona in those years. In 1954 they laid the cornerstone of Nou Camp, the great Barcelona stadium built for Kubala: the old stadium couldn't hold the multitude that came to cheer his precision passes and deadly blasts. Czibor, meanwhile, struck sparks from his shoes. The other Hungarian at Barcelona, Kocsis, was a great header. "Head of Gold," they called him, and a sea of handkerchiefs celebrated his goals. They said Kocsis had the best head in Europe after Churchill.

Earlier on, in 1950, Kubala formed a Hungarian team in exile, and that earned him a two-year suspension from FIFA. For playing on another exile team after Soviet tanks crushed the uprising at the end of 1956, FIFA suspended Puskas, Czibor, Kocsis and other Hungarians for over a year.

In 1958, in the midst of its war of independence, Algeria formed a soccer team which for the first time wore the national colors. Its line was made up of Makhloufi, Ben Tifour and other Algerians who were professional players in France.

Blockaded by the colonial power, Algeria only managed to play against Morocco—who was then kicked out of FIFA for several years for committing such a sin—and engage in several unimportant games organized by sports unions in some Arab and Eastern European countries. FIFA slammed all the doors on the Algerian team, and the French soccer league blacklisted the players. Imprisoned by contracts, they were barred from ever returning to professional activity.

But after Algeria won its independence, the French had no alternative but to call up the players the fans longed for.

the blacks

IN 1916, in the first South American championship, Uruguay beat Chile 4–0. The next day, the Chilean delegation insisted the game be disallowed, "because Uruguay had two Africans in the lineup." They were Isabelino Gradín and Juan Delgado. Gradín had scored two of the four goals.

Gradín was born in Montevideo, the great-grandson of slaves: he was a man who lifted people out of their seats when he erupted with astonishing speed, dominating the ball as easily as if he were walking, and without a pause, he'd drive past the adversaries and score on the fly. He had a face like the holy host and was one of those guys who no one believes when they pretend to be bad.

Juan Delgado, also a great-grandson of slaves, was born in the town of Florida, in the Uruguayan countryside. Delgado liked to show off by dancing with a broom at carnival and with the ball on the field. He talked while he played, and he'd tease his opponents: "Pick me that bunch of grapes," he'd say as he sent the ball high. And as he shot he'd tell the keeper: "Jump for it, the sand is soft."

Back then, Uruguay was the only country in the world with black players on its national team.

zamora

HE MADE his first division début when he was sixteen, still wearing short pants. Before taking the field with Español in Barcelona, he put on a high-necked English shirt, gloves and a hard cap like a helmet to protect himself from the sun and other blows. The year was 1917 and the attacks were like cavalry charges. Ricardo Zamora had chosen a high-risk career. The only one in greater danger than the goalkeeper was the referee, known at that time as "The Nazarene," because the fields had no dugouts or fences to protect him from the vengeance of the fans. Each goal gave rise to a long hiatus while people ran onto the playing field either to embrace or throw punches.

Over the years, the image of Zamora in those clothes became famous. He sowed panic among strikers. If they looked his way they were lost: with Zamora in the goal, the net would shrink and the posts would lose themselves in the distance.

They called him "The Divine One." For twenty years, he was the best goalkeeper in the world. He liked cognac and smoked three packs a day, plus the occasional cigar.

samitier

LIKE SAMORA, Josep Samitier made his début in the first division when he was sixteen. In 1918 he signed with Barcelona in exchange for a watch with a dial that glowed in the dark, something he'd never seen, and a suit with a waistcoat.

A short time later, he was the team's ace and his biography was on newsstands all over the city. His name was on the lips of cabaret *chanteuses*, bandied about on the stage and revered in sports columns where they praised the "Mediterranean style" invented by Zamora and Samitier.

Samitier, a striker with a devastating shot, stood out for his cleverness, his domination of the ball, his utter lack of respect for the rules of logic, and his Olympian scorn for the borders of space and time.

death on the field

ABDÓN PORTE, who wore the shirt of the Uruguayan club Nacional for more than two hundred games in four years, always drew applause and sometimes cheers, until his lucky star fell.

They took him out of the starting line-up. He waited, asked to return and did. But it was no use, the slump continued, the crowd whistled: on the defense even tortoises got past him, on the attack he couldn't score a single goal.

At the end of the summer of 1918, in the Nacional stadium, Abdón Porte killed himself. He shot himself at midnight at the center of the field where he had been loved. All the lights were out. No one heard the gunshot.

They found him at dawn. In one hand he held a revolver and in the other a letter.

friedenreich

IN 1919, Brazil defeated Uruguay 1-0 and crowned itself champion of South America. People flooded the streets of Rio de Janeiro. Leading the celebration, raised aloft like a standard, was a muddy soccer boot with a little sign that proclaimed: "The glorious foot of Friedenreich." The next day that boot, which had scored the winning goal, ended up in the display window of a downtown jewelery shop.

Artur Friedenreich, son of a German immigrant and a black washerwoman, played in the first division for twenty-six years and never earned a cent. No one scored more goals than he in the history of soccer, not even that other great Brazilian artilleryman, Pelé, who remains professional soccer's leading scorer. Friedenreich accumulated 1,329, Pelé 1,279.

This green-eyed mulatto founded the Brazilian style of play. He, or the devil who got into him through the sole of his foot, broke all the rules in the English manuals: Friedenreich brought to the solemn stadium of the whites the irreverence of brown boys who entertained themselves fighting over a rag ball in the slums. Thus was born a style open to fantasy, one which prefers pleasure to results. From Friedenreich onward, there have been no right angles in Brazilian soccer, just as there are none in the mountains of Rio de Janeiro or the buildings of Oscar Niemeyer.

from mutilation to splendor

IN 1921 the South American Cup was played in Buenos Aires. The president of Brazil, Epitácio Pessoa, issued a decree: for reasons of patriotic prestige there would be no brown skin on Brazil's national team. Of the three games they played, the white team lost two.

Friedenreich did not play in that championship tournament. It was impossible to be black in Brazilian soccer, and being mulatto wasn't easy either. Friedenreich always started late because it took him half an hour to iron his hair in the dressing room. The only mulatto player on Fluminense, Carlos Alberto, used to whiten his face with rice powder.

Later on, despite the owners of power, things began to change. With the passage of time, the old soccer mutilated by racism gave way to the splendor of its diverse colors. And after so many years it is obvious that Brazil's best players, from Friedenreich to Romario, by way of Domingos da Guía, Leónidas, Zizinho, Garrincha, Didí and Pelé, have always been blacks and mulattos. All of them came up from poverty, and some of them returned to it. By contrast, there have never been blacks or mulattos among Brazil's car-racing champions. Like tennis, it is a sport that requires money.

In the global social pyramid, blacks are at the bottom and whites are at the top. In Brazil this is called "racial democracy," but in fact soccer is one of very few democratic venues where people of color can now compete on an equal footing. Equal up to a point, because even in soccer some are more equal than others. They all have the same rights, but the player who grew up hungry and the athlete who never missed a meal don't really compete on a level playing field. But at least soccer offers a shot at social mobility for a poor child, usually black or mulatto, who had no other toy but a ball. The ball is the only fairy godmother he can believe in. Maybe she will feed him, maybe she will make him a hero, maybe even a god.

Misery trains him for soccer or for crime. From the moment of birth, that child is forced to turn his disadvantage into a weapon, and before long he learns to dribble around the rules of order which deny him a place. He learns the tricks of every trade and he becomes an expert in the art of pretending, surprising, breaking through where least expected, and throwing off an enemy with a hip feint or some other tune from the rascal's songbook.

the second discovery of america

FOR PEDRO ARISPE, homeland meant nothing. It was the place where he was born, which meant nothing to him because he had no choice in the matter, and that was where he broke his back working as a peon for a man who was the same as any boss in any country. But when Uruguay won the 1924 Olympic title in France, Arispe was one of the winning players. While he watched the flag with the sun and four pale-blue stripes rising slowly up the pole of honor, at the center of all the flags and higher than any other, Arispe felt his heart burst.

Four years later, Uruguay won the Olympic final in Holland. And a prominent Uruguayan, Atilio Narancio, who in '24 had mortgaged his house to pay for the players' passage, commented: "We are no longer just a tiny spot on the map of the world."

The sky-blue shirt was proof of the existence of the nation: Uruguay was not a mistake. Soccer pulled this tiny country out of the shadows of universal anonymity.

The authors of those miracles of '24 and '28 were workers and wanderers who got nothing from soccer but the pleasure of playing. Pedro Arispe was a meat-packer. José Nasazzi cut marble. "Perucho" Petrone worked for a grocer. Pedro Cea sold ice. José Leandro Andrade was a carnival musician and bootblack. They were all twenty years old, more or less, though in the pictures they look like senior citizens. They cured their wounds with salt water, vinegar plasters and a few glasses of wine.

In 1924, they arrived in Europe in third-class steerage and then travelled on borrowed money in second-class carriages, sleeping on wooden benches and playing game after game in exchange for room and board. Before the Paris Olympics, they played nine games in Spain and won all of them.

It was the first time that a Latin American team had played in Europe. The first match was against Yugoslavia. The Yugoslavs sent spies to the practice session. The Uruguayans caught on and practiced by kicking the ground and sending the ball up into the clouds, tripping at every step and crashing into each other. The spies reported: "It makes you feel sorry, these poor boys came from so far away. . . "

Barely two thousand fans watched the game. The Uruguayan flag was flown upside down, the sun on its head, and instead of the national anthem they played a Brazilian march. That afternoon, Uruguay defeated Yugoslavia 7-0.

And then something like the second discovery of America occurred. Game after game, the crowd jostled to see those men, slippery like squirrels, who played chess with a ball. The English squad had perfected the long pass and the high ball, but these disinherited children from far-off America didn't walk in their fathers' footsteps. They chose to invent a game of close passes directly to the foot, with lightning changes in rhythm and high-speed dribbling. Henri de Montherlant, an aristocratic writer, published his enthusiasm: "A revelation! Here we have real soccer. Compared with this, what we knew before, what we played, was no more than a schoolboy's hobby."

Uruguay's success at the '24 and '28 Olympics, and at the 1930 and 1950 World Cups, owed a large debt to the government's policy of building sports fields around the country to promote physical education. Now all that remains of the state's social calling, and of soccer, is nostalgia. Several players, like the very subtle Enzo Francescoli, have managed to inherit and renovate the old arts, but in general Uruguayan soccer is a far cry from what it used to be. Ever fewer children play it and ever fewer men play it gracefully. Nevertheless, there is no Uruguayan who does not consider himself a Ph.D. in tactics and strategy, and a scholar of its history. Uruguayans' passion for soccer comes from those days long ago, and its deep roots are still visible. Every time the national team plays, no matter against whom, the country holds its breath. Politicians, singers and street vendors shut their mouths, lovers suspend their caresses, and flies stop flying.

andrade

EUROPE HAD never seen a black man play soccer.

In the '24 Olympics, the Uruguayan José Leandro Andrade dazzled everyone with his exquisite plays. A midfielder, this rubber-bodied giant would sweep the ball downfield without ever touching an adversary, and when he launched the attack he would brandish his body and send them all scattering. In one match he crossed half the field with the ball sitting on his head. The crowds cheered him, the French press called him "The Black Marvel."

When the tournament was over, Andrade spent some time hanging around Paris, where he was an errant bohemian and king of the cabarets. Patent leather shoes replaced his whiskery hemp sandals from Montevideo and a top hat took the place of his worn cap. Newspaper columns of the time praised the image of that monarch of the Pigalle night: gay jaunty step, over-sized grin, half-closed eyes always staring into the distance. And dressed to kill: silk handkerchief, striped jacket, bright yellow gloves and a cane with a silver handle.

Andrade died in Montevideo many years later. His friends had planned several benefits for him, but none of them ever came off. He died of tuberculosis, in utter poverty.

He was black, South American and poor, the first international soccer idol.

ringlets

THEY CALLED the successive figure-eights Uruguayan players drew on the field *moñas*, or ringlets. French journalists wanted the secret of the witchcraft that cast the rival players in stone. Through an interpreter, José Leandro Andrade revealed the formula: the players trained by chasing chickens that fled making S's on the ground. The reporters believed it and published the story.

Many years later, good ringlets were still cheered as loudly as goals in South American soccer. My childhood memory is filled with them. I close my eyes and I see, for example, Walter Gómez, that dizzying bushwacker who'd dive into the swamp of enemy legs and with ringlet after ringlet leave a wake of fallen bodies. The stands would confess:

We'd all rather fast
than miss a Walter Gómez pass.

He liked to knead the ball, retain it and caress it, and if it got away from him, he'd feel insulted. No coach would dare tell him, as they say now: "If you want to knead, go work in a bakery."

The ringlet wasn't just a bit of tolerated mischief, it was a joy the crowd demanded. Today such works of art are outlawed, or at least viewed with grave suspicion as selfish exhibitionism, a betrayal of team spirit, and utterly useless against the iron defensive systems of modern soccer.

the olympic goal

WHEN THE Uruguayan team returned from the '24 Olympics, the Argentines challenged them to a friendly game. The match was played in Buenos Aires. Uruguay lost by one goal.

Left wing Cesáreo Onzari was the creator of the winning goal. He took a corner and the ball went directly into the net without anyone else touching it. It was the first time in the history of soccer a goal was scored that way. The Uruguayans were left speechless. When they found their tongues, they protested. They claimed the goalkeeper, Mazali, was pushed when the ball was in the air. The referee wouldn't listen. Then they howled that Onzari hadn't intended to shoot at the net and that the goal had been scored by the wind.

In homage or in irony, that rarity became known in South America as the "Olympic goal." It's still called that, on the rare occasions it occurs. Onzari spent the rest of his life swearing it wasn't by chance. And though years have gone by, the mistrust continues: every time a corner shakes the net without intermediaries, the crowd celebrates the goal with a cheer, but doesn't quite believe it.

goal by piendibene

IT WAS 1926. The scorer, José Piendibene, didn't celebrate. Piendibene, a man of rare mastery and rarer modesty, never celebrated his goals, so as not to offend.

The Uruguayan club Peñarol was playing in Montevideo against Español of Barcelona, and they couldn't find a way to penetrate the goal defended by Zamora. The play came from behind. Anselmo slipped around two adversaries, sent the ball across to Suffiati and then took off expecting a pass back. But Piendibene asked for it. He caught the pass, eluded Urquizú and closed in on the goal. Zamora saw that Piendibene was shooting for the right corner and he leapt to block it. The ball hadn't moved, she was asleep on his foot: Piendibene tossed her softly to the left side of the empty net. Zamora managed to jump back, a cat's leap, and grazed the ball with his fingertips when it was already too late.

the bicycle kick

RAMÓN UNZAGA invented the move on the field of the Chilean port Talcahuana: body in the air, back to the ground, he shot the ball backwards with a sudden snap of his legs, like the blades of scissors.

It was some years later when this acrobatic act came to be called the "chilena," in 1927 when Colo-Colo travelled to Europe and striker David Arellano performed it in Spanish stadiums. Journalists cheered the splendor of this unknown gambol, and they baptized it "chilena" because, like strawberries and the cueca, it had come from Chile.

After several flying goals, Arellano died that year, in the stadium at Valladolid, killed in a fatal encounter with a fullback.

scarone

FORTY YEARS before the Brazilians Pelé and Coutinho, the Uruguayans Scarone and Cea rolled over the rival's defense with zigzag passes that went back and forth from one to the other all the way to the goal, yours and mine, close and right to the foot, question and response, response and question: the ball rebounded without a moment's pause, as if off a wall.

That's what they called that River Plate style of attack back in those days, "The Wall."

Héctor Scarone served up passes like offerings and scored goals with a marksmanship he sharpened during practice sessions by knocking over bottles at thirty meters. And though he was rather short, when it came to jumping he was up long before the rest. Scarone knew how to float in the air, breaking the law of gravity. He would leap for the ball, break free of his adversaries and spin about like a top to face the goal. And then, still in the air, he would head it in.

They called him "The Magician" because he pulled goals out of a hat, and they also called him "The Gardel of Soccer," because while he played he sang like no one else.

goal by scarone

IT WAS 1928, during the Olympic final.

Uruguay and Argentina were tied when Píriz shot the ball across to Tarasconi and advanced toward the penalty area. Borjas met the ball with his back to the goal and headed it to Scarone, screaming, "Yours, Héctor!" and Scarone kicked it sharply on the fly. The Argentine goalkeeper, Bossio, dove for it but it had already hit the net. The ball bounced defiantly back onto the field. Uruguayan striker Figueroa sent it in

again, punishing the ball with a swift kick, because leaving
the goal like that was bad form.

the occult forces

A URUGUAYAN player, Adhemar Canavessi, sacrificed himself
to avert the damage his presence would have caused in the
final match of the '28 Olympics in Amsterdam. Uruguay was
to play Argentina. Every time Canavessi had faced the
Argentines, Uruguay had lost, and last time he had had the
bad luck to score a goal against his own side. He got off the
bus taking the players to the stadium. In Amsterdam, without
Canavessi, Uruguay won.

The previous day, Carlos Gardel had sung for the
Argentine players at the hotel where they were staying. To
bring them luck, he'd brought out a new tango called "Dandy."
Two years later, just before the final of the 1930 World Cup, it
happened again: Gardel sang "Dandy" to wish the team success
and Uruguay won the final. Many swear his intentions were
beyond reproach, but there are those who believe therein lies
the proof that Gardel was Uruguayan.

goal by nolo

IT WAS 1929. Argentina was playing Paraguay.

Nolo Ferreira brought the ball up from right at the back. He broke open a path, leaving a string of fallen bodies, until he suddenly found himself face to face with the entire defense lined up in a wall. Then Nolo stopped. He stood there passing the ball from one foot to the other, from one instep to the other, not letting it touch the ground. His adversaries tilted their heads from left to right and right to left, in unison, hypnotized, their gaze fixed on that pendulum of a ball. The back-and-forth went on for centuries, until Nolo found a hole and shot without warning: the ball pierced the wall and shook the net.

The mounted police got off their horses to congratulate him. Twenty thousand people were on the field, but every Argentine will swear he was there.

the 1930 world cup

AN EARTHQUAKE was shaking the south of Italy and burying 1,500 Neapolitans, Marlene Dietrich was singing "Blue Angel," Stalin was completing his usurpation of the Russian Revolution, the poet Vladimir Mayakovski was committing suicide. The English were jailing Mahatma Gandhi, who by demanding independence and loving his country had brought India to a standstill; under the same banner in the other Indies, our Indies, Augusto César Sandino was rousing the peasants of Nicaragua and U.S. Marines were burning the crops to defeat him by hunger.

In the United States some were dancing the new boogie-woogie, but the euphoria of the Roaring Twenties had been knocked out cold by the ferocious blows of the crisis of '29. When the New York Stock Exchange crashed, it devastated international commodity prices and dragged several Latin American governments into the abyss. The price of tin took a nosedive, pulling Bolivian President Hernando Siles after it and putting a general in his place, while the collapse of meat and wheat prices finished President Hipólito Yrigoyen in Argentina and installed another general in his place. In the Dominican Republic, the fall in sugar prices opened the long cycle of dictatorship of General Rafael Leónidas Trujillo, who was then inaugurating his regime by baptizing the capital city and the port with his own name.

In Uruguay, the coup d'etat was not to strike until three years later. In 1930, the country had eyes and ears only for the first World Cup. Uruguayan victories in the previous two Olympics made the country the obvious choice to host the first tournament.

Twelve nations arrived at the port of Montevideo. Every European country was invited, but only four teams crossed the ocean to these southern shores: "That's far away from everything," it was said, "and the passage is expensive."

A ship brought the Jules Rimet trophy from France, accompanied by FIFA president Don Jules himself and by the reluctant French team.

With pomp and circumstance Uruguay inaugurated the monumental showcase it had taken eight months to build. The stadium was called Centenario, to celebrate the constitution which a century before had denied civil rights to women, the illiterate and the poor. There wasn't room for a pin in the stands when Uruguay and Argentina faced each other in the final. The stadium was a sea of felt hats and canopies over cameras with tripods. The goalkeepers wore caps and the referee wore black plus-fours.

The final of the 1930 World Cup did not merit more than a twenty-line column in the Italian daily *La Gazzetta dello Sport.* After all, it was a repeat of the Amsterdam Olympics in 1928: the two nations of the River Plate insulted Europe by showing the world where the best soccer was played. As in '28, Argentina took second place. Uruguay, losing 2-1 at half-time, ended up winning 4–2 and was crowned champion. To referee the final, the Belgian John Langenus demanded life insurance, but nothing more serious occurred than a few tussles in the stands. Afterwards, in Buenos Aires, a crowd stoned the Uruguayan consulate.

Third place went to the United States, who had among its players several recent Scottish immigrants, and fourth place went to Yugoslavia.

Not a single match ended in a draw. The Argentine Stábile headed up the list of scorers with eight goals, followed by the Uruguayan Cea with five. Louis Laurent of France scored the first goal in World Cup history, against Mexico.

nasazzi

NOT EVEN X-rays could get through him. They called him "The Terrible."

"The field is a jar," he'd say. "And the mouth of the jar is the penalty area."

There, in the box, he was boss.

José Nasazzi, captain of the Uruguayan teams of '24, '28 and '30, was the first caudillo of Uruguayan soccer. He was the windmill of the entire team, which worked to the rhythm of his shouts of warning, disappointment and encouragement. No one ever heard him complain.

camus

IN 1930, Albert Camus was Saint Peter guarding the gate for the University of Algeria's soccer team. He had been playing goalkeeper since he was a child, because in that position your shoes don't wear out as fast. From a poor home, Camus couldn't afford the luxury of running the fields; every night, his grandmother examined the soles of his shoes and gave him a beating if she found them worn.

During his years in the net, Camus learned many things: "I learned that the ball never comes where you expect it to.

That helped me a lot in life, especially in large cities where people don't tend to be what they claim."

He also learned to win without feeling like God and to lose without feeling like rubbish, skills not easily acquired, and he learned to unravel several mysteries of the human soul, whose labyrinths he explored later on in a dangerous journey on the page.

juggernauts

ONE OF the world-champion Uruguayans, "Perucho" Petrone, packed up and moved to Italy. The afternoon in 1931 when Petrone made his début for Fiorentina, he scored eleven goals.

He didn't last long in Italy. He was the top scorer in the Italian championship and Fiorentina offered him everything, but Petrone tired quickly of the hurrahs of fascism on the rise. Fed up and nostalgic, he went back to Montevideo where for a while he continued scoring his scorched-earth goals. He wasn't yet thirty when he had to leave soccer for good. FIFA forced him out because he broke his contract with Fiorentina.

They say Petrone's shot could knock down a wall. Who knows? One thing's for sure: it knocked out goalkeepers and broke through nets.

Meanwhile, on the other shore of the River Plate, the Argentine Bernabé Ferreyra was also shooting cannonballs with the fury of the possessed. Fans from every team went to see "The Wild Animal" start out deep, cut his way through the defense and put the ball in the net and the keeper along with it.

Before and after each game and at half-time as well, they would play a tango over the loudspeakers composed in homage to Bernabé's artillery barrages. In 1932, the newspaper *Crítica* offered a sizable prize to the goalkeeper who could stop him from scoring. One afternoon that year, Bernabé had to take off his shoes for a group of journalists to prove no iron bars were hidden in the toes.

professionalism

EVEN THOUGH recent scandals—"clean hands, clean feet"—have put the bosses of Italy's biggest clubs on the spot, soccer is still among the country's ten most important industries, and the country remains a magnet for South American players.

Italy was already a Mecca way back in the times of Mussolini. Nowhere else in the world did they pay so well. Players would threaten owners with, "I'm going to Italy," and those magic words would loosen the purse strings. Some really did go, travelling by ship from Buenos Aires, Montevideo, São Paulo and Rio de Janeiro, and if they didn't have Italian parents or grandparents somebody in Rome would invent a family on the spot for immediate citizenship.

The exodus of players was one factor that led to the birth of professional soccer in our countries. In 1931 Argentina turned pro, and Uruguay followed suit the next year. In Brazil a professional league was launched in 1934. That was when they legalized payments previously made under the table, and the player became a worker. The contract tied him to the club full time and for life, and he could not change his workplace unless the team sold him. Like a factory worker, the player traded his energy for a wage and became as much a prisoner on the field as a serf was on a manor. But in the early days the demands of professional soccer weren't great—only two hours a week of obligatory training. In Argentina anyone missing a practice session without a doctor's note paid a five-peso fine.

the 1934 world cup

JOHNNY WEISSMULLER was doing his first Tarzan howl, the first mass-produced deodorant was hitting the market, and Louisiana police were shooting down Bonnie and Clyde.

Bolivia and Paraguay, the two poorest countries in South America, were fighting in the names of Standard Oil and Shell and bleeding over oil in the Chaco. Sandino, having defeated the marines in Nicaragua, was shot dead in an ambush and Somoza, the murderer, was inaugurating his dynasty. In China, Mao was beginning his Long March. In Germany, Hitler was being crowned Führer of the Third Reich and was promulgating the Law for the Defense of the Aryan Race, which forced sterilization on criminals and on anyone with a hereditary disease. And in Italy, Mussolini was inaugurating the second World Cup.

Posters for the championship showed Hercules balancing a ball on his foot while doing the fascist salute. For Il Duce, the '34 World Cup in Rome was an elaborate propaganda operation. Mussolini attended all the games, sitting in the box of honor, his chin raised toward stands filled with black shirts. The eleven players of the Italian team dedicated their victories to him, their right arms outstretched.

But the road to the title wasn't easy. The semi-final between Italy and Spain turned out to be the most grueling match in the history of the World Cup. The battle lasted 210 minutes and didn't end until the following day. Italy won, but finished without four of their starting players and Spain without seven of theirs, sidelined by war-wounds or sheer exhaustion. Among the wounded Spaniards were the two best players: Lángara and the keeper Zamora, who hypnotized anyone who set foot in the box.

Italy waged the final against Czechoslovakia in the National Fascist Party Stadium and won 2-1. Two Argentines recently nationalized as Italians did their part: Orsi scored the first goal, dribbling around the goalkeeper, and the other Argentine, Guaita, made a pass to Schiavio to set up the goal that gave Italy its first World Cup.

In '34 sixteen countries participated: twelve from Europe, three from Latin America, and Egypt, the lone representative of the rest of the world. The reigning champion, Uruguay, refused to go because Italy hadn't come to the first World Cup in Montevideo.

Germany and Austria came in third and fourth. The Czech Nejedly was the leading scorer with five goals, followed by Cohen from Germany and Schiavio from Italy with four apiece.

god and the devil in rio de janeiro

ONE VERY rainy night while the year 1937 was dying, an enemy fan buried a toad with its mouth sewn shut in Vasco da Gama's playing field and called down a curse: "Vasco won't win a championship for the next twelve years! They won't, if there is a God in heaven!" He was a fan of a humble team that Vasco da Gama had beaten 12-0; Arubinha was his name.

For years, fans and players alike searched for that toad on and around the field. They never found it. The playing field was so pockmarked, it looked like a moonscape. Vasco da Gama hired the best players in Brazil, put together sides that were veritable powerhouses, but they kept on losing.

At last, in 1945, the team won the Rio trophy and broke the curse. They hadn't been champions since 1934. Eleven years of drought. "God gave us a little discount," the club president commented.

Much later, in 1953, it was Flamengo that had problems, the most popular club not only in Rio de Janeiro but in all Brazil, the only club that's the home team wherever it plays. Their fans, who are the most numerous and fervent in the world, were dying of hunger. Then a Catholic priest, one Father Goes, offered a guarantee of victory as long as the players attended his mass before each game and said the rosary kneeling before the altar.

Flamengo won the cup three years in a row. Their rivals protested to Cardinal Jaime Câmara: Flamengo was using outlawed weapons. Father Goes defended himself claiming all he did was show them the way of the Lord. The players continued saying their rosaries of black and red beads, colors which are not only Flamengo's but those of an African deity who incarnates Jesus and Satan at the same time. In the fourth year, Flamengo lost the championship. The players stopped going to mass and never said the rosary again. Father Goes asked the Pope for help, but he never answered.

Father Romualdo, on the other hand, obtained the Pope's permission to become a partner in Fluminense. The priest attended every practice session. The players didn't like it one bit. Twelve years had passed since Fluminense last won the

Rio trophy and it was bad luck to have that big black bird standing at the edge of the field. The players shouted insults at him, unaware that Father Romualdo had been deaf since birth.

One fine day, Fluminense started to win. They won one championship, then another and another. Now the players would only practice in the shadow of Father Romualdo. After every goal they kissed his cassock. On weekends the priest watched the games from the box of honor and babbled who knows what against the referee and the opposing players.

the sources of misfortune

EVERYONE KNOWS it's bad luck to step on a toad or on the shadow of a tree, to walk under a ladder, to sit or sleep backwards, to open an umbrella indoors, to count your teeth or to break a mirror. But in soccer that barely scratches the surface.

Carlos Bilardo, coach of the Argentine team for the World Cup in 1986 and 1990, didn't let his players eat chicken because it brings bad luck and he made them eat beef, which brings uric acid.

Silvio Berlusconi, owner of Milan, forbade fans from singing the club's anthem, the traditional chant "Milan, Milan," because its malevolent vibrations paralyzed his players' legs; in 1987 he commissioned a new anthem, "Milan dei nostri cuori."

Freddy Rincón, Colombia's black giant, disappointed his many admirers in the '94 World Cup. He played without a drop of enthusiasm. Afterwards we learned that it wasn't from a lack of desire, but an excess of fear. A prophet from Buenaventura, Rincón's home on the Colombian coast, had foretold the results of the championship, which turned out exactly as predicted, and warned that he would break his leg if he was not very careful. "Watch out for the girl with freckles," he said, referring to the ball, "and for the one with hepatitis, and the one covered in blood," alluding to the yellow and red cards of the referee.

On the eve of that Cup's final, Italian specialists in the occult declared their country would win. "Numerous evil spirits from black magic will keep Brazil from winning," the Italian Magicians Association assured the press. The result did not add to the prestige of that professional association.

amulets and spells

MANY PLAYERS put their right foot first and cross themselves when they step onto the field. There are also some who go directly to the empty goal and kick one in, or kiss the posts. Others touch the grass and bring their fingers to their lips.

Often you see a player wearing a little medal around his neck or some magic band tied around his wrist. If his penalty kick goes awry, it's because someone spat on the ball. If he misses an easy shot, it's because a witch closed the enemy goal. If he loses the match, it's because he gave away his shirt after the last victory.

Amadeo Carrizo, goalkeeper for the Argentine club River Plate, went eight games with his net untouched thanks to the powers of a cap he wore day and night. That cap exorcised the demons of the goal. One afternoon Angel Clemente Rojas, a player for Boca Juniors, stole it. Without his amulet, Carrizo let in two goals and River lost the match.

A leading Spanish player, Pablo Hernández Coronado, says that when Real Madrid refurbished its stadium the team didn't win a championship for six years, until a fan broke the curse by burying a head of garlic in the center of the playing field. Barcelona's celebrated forward Luis Suárez didn't believe in curses, but he knew that every time he knocked over a glass of wine while eating he was going to score a few goals.

To invoke the evil spirits of defeat, fans throw salt on the enemy's playing field. To scare them off, they sow their own field with fistfuls of wheat or rice. Others light candles, offer the earth cane liquor or toss flowers into the sea. Some fans seek protection by praying to Jesus of Nazareth and the blessed souls who died by fire, drowning or losing their way. In several places Saint George's lances and those of his African twin Ogum have proved very effective against the dragon of the evil eye.

Thoughtful gestures are appreciated. Fans favored by the gods crawl on their knees up steep slopes, wrapped in the team flag, or they spend the rest of their days whispering the million rosaries they swore to say. When Botafogo was crowned champion in 1957, Didí left the field without going to the dressing room and, still in his uniform, he fulfilled the promise he had made to his patron saint: he walked across the city of Rio de Janeiro, from end to end.

But deities do not always have time to come to the aid of soccer players tormented by misfortune. The Mexican team arrived at the 1930 World Cup overwhelmed by pessimistic predictions. Just before the match against France, Mexican coach Juan Luqué de Serrallonga gave the players a pep talk at his hotel in Montevideo. He assured them that the Virgin of Guadalupe was praying for them back home on Tepeyac Hill.

The coach wasn't appraised of the Virgin's busy schedule. France scored four goals and Mexico finished in last place.

erico

DURING THE Chaco war, while the peasants of Bolivia and Paraguay were marching to the slaughter, Paraguay's soccer players were in other countries playing to raise money for those who fell helplessly wounded in a desert where no birds sang and people left no footprints. That's how Arsenio Erico got to Buenos Aires, and in Buenos Aires he stayed. Argentina's leading scorer of all time was Paraguayan. Erico scored over forty goals a season.

He had secret springs hidden in his body. That magician could jump without bending his knees and his head always reached higher than the goalkeeper's hands. The more relaxed his legs seemed, the more powerfully they would explode to lash out at the goal. Often Erico would whip it in with his heel. There was no deadlier backheel in the history of soccer.

When Erico wasn't scoring goals, he was offering them on a platter to his teammates. Cátulo Castillo dedicated a tango to him:

> *Your pass from the heel or head is such*
> *a marvelous feat*
> *a thousand years won't see a repeat.*

And he did it with the elegance of a dancer. "He's Nijinski," commented the French writer Paul Morand when he saw him play.

the 1938 world cup

MAX THEILER was discovering a vaccine for yellow fever, color photography was being born, Walt Disney was launching "Snow White," and Eisenstein was filming "Alexander Nevski." Nylon, invented not long before by a Harvard professor, was being turned into parachutes and ladies' stockings.

The Argentine poets Alfonsina Storni and Leopoldo Lugones were killing themselves. Lázaro Cárdenas was nationalizing Mexico's oil and confronting a blockade and other Western furies. Orson Welles was broadcasting a Martian invasion of the United States to frighten the gullible, while Standard Oil was demanding a real invasion of Mexico to punish the heresy of Cárdenas and put an end to his bad example.

In Italy, *Manifesto on the Race* was being written and anti-Semitic attacks were on the rise. Germany was occupying Austria; Hitler was hunting down Jews and devouring territory. The English government was ordering its people to stockpile food and teaching them to defend themselves against poison gas. Franco was cornering the last bastions of the Spanish Republic and receiving the recognition of the Vatican. César Vallejo was dying in Paris, probably in the pouring rain, while Sartre was publishing *Nausea*. And there, in Paris, under the darkening shadows of the war to come, where Picasso's "Guernica" was on display to denounce the time of infamy, the third World Cup got underway. In Colombes stadium, French president Albert Lebrun made the ceremonial kick-off: he aimed at the ball, but cuffed the ground.

As with the previous Cup, this was a European championship. Only two South American countries joined eleven European ones. A team from Indonesia, still called the Dutch East Indies, came to Paris as the sole representative of the rest of the planet.

Germany's side incorporated five players from recently annexed Austria. Thus reinforced, with swastikas on their chests and all the Nazi symbols of power to hand, the German squad came on strong, claiming invincibility, only to trip and fall to modest Switzerland. The German defeat occurred a few days before Aryan supremacy suffered another rude blow in New York, when black boxer Joe Louis pulverized German champion Max Schmeling.

Italy, on the other hand, pulled off a repeat of the previous World Cup. In the semi-final, the *Azzurri* defeated Brazil. One penalty was questionable, but Brazil protested in vain. As in '34, all the referees were European.

Then came the final: Italy against Hungary. For Mussolini, winning was a matter of state. On the eve of the game, the Italian players received a three-word telegram from Rome, signed by the fascist chief: "Win or die." They didn't have to die because Italy won 4-2. The following day the victors wore military uniforms to the final ceremony, presided over by Il Duce.

La Gazzetta dello Sport exalted "the apotheosis of fascist sports symbolized by this victory of the race." Not long before, the official press had celebrated Italy's defeat of Brazil with these words: "We salute the triumph of Italic intelligence over the brute force of the Negroes."

But it was the international press who chose the best players of the tournament, and among them were two black men, Brazilians Leônidas and Domingos da Guia. With eight goals Leônidas was also the leading scorer, followed by the Hungarian Zsengeller with seven. The most beautiful goal scored by Leônidas was against Poland. Playing in a torrential storm, he lost his shoe in the mud of the penalty area and scored the goal barefoot.

goal by meazza

IT WAS at the World Cup in '38. In the semi-final, Italy and Brazil were risking their necks for all or nothing.

Italian striker Piola suddenly collapsed as if he'd been shot, and with the last flutter of life in his finger he pointed at Brazilian defender Domingos da Guia. The referee believed him and blew the whistle: penalty. While the Brazilians screamed to high heaven and Piola got up and dusted himself off, Giusepe Meazza placed the ball on the firing point.

Meazza was the dandy of the picture. A short, handsome, Latin lover and an elegant artilleryman of penalties, he lifted his chin to the goalkeeper like a matador before the final charge. His feet, as soft and knowing as hands, never missed. But Walter, the Brazilian goalie, was good at blocking penalty kicks and felt confident.

Meazza began his run up, and just when he was about to execute the kick, he dropped his shorts. The crowd was stupefied and the referee nearly swallowed his whistle. But Meazza, never pausing, grabbed his pants with one hand and sent the goalkeeper, disarmed by laughter, down to defeat.

That was the goal that put Italy in the final.

leônidas

HE HAD the dimensions, speed and cunning of a mosquito. In the '38 World Cup a journalist from *Paris Match* counted six legs on him and suggested black magic was responsible. I don't know if the journalist noticed, but Leônidas's many legs had the diabolical ability to grow several yards and fold over or tie themselves in knots.

Leônidas da Silva stepped onto the field the day Artur Friedenreich, already in his forties, retired. He received the scepter from the old master. It wasn't long before they named a brand of cigarettes and a candy bar after him. He got more fan letters than a movie star: the letters asked him for a picture, an autograph or a government job.

Leônidas scored many goals, but never counted them. A few were made from the air, his feet twirling, upside down, back to the goal. He was skilled in the acrobatics of the "chilena," which Brazilians call the bicycle.

Leônidas's goals were so pretty that even the goalkeeper would get up and congratulate him.

domingos

TO THE EAST, the Great Wall of China. To the west, Domingos da Guia.

In the entire history of soccer no fullback was more solid. Domingos was champion in four cities—Rio de Janeiro, São Paulo, Montevideo and Buenos Aires—and he was adored by all four: when he played, the stadiums were always full.

Fullbacks used to stick like stamps to strikers and peel off the ball as quickly as possible, wafting it to high heaven before it burned their feet. Domingos, however, let his adversaries stampede by vainly while he stole the ball; then he would take all the time in the world to bring it out of the box. A man of imperturbable style, he was always whistling and looking the other way. He scorned speed. He would play in slow motion, master of suspense, lover of leisure: the art of bringing the ball out of the box slowly, calmly, was baptized *domingada.* When he finally let the ball go, he did so without ever running and without wanting to, because it saddened him to be left without her.

domingos and she

THIS BALL here helped me a lot. She or her sisters, right? It's a family to whom I owe a debt of gratitude. In my time on earth, she was the key. Because without her nobody plays at all. I started out in the Bangú factory. Working, working, until I met my friend here. And I was very happy with her.

I've seen the world, traveled a lot, had many women. Women are a pleasure too, right?

(Testimony collected by Roberto Moura)

goal by atilio

IT WAS 1939. Nacional from Montevideo and Boca Juniors from Buenos Aires were tied at two goals apiece, and time was running out. Nacional was on the attack; Boca, in retreat, was holding them off. Then Atilio García got the ball, faced the jungle of legs, and opened up a path on the right, gobbling up the field, adversary by adversary.

Atilio was used to getting kicked. They'd go after him with everything they had, his legs were a map of scars. That afternoon on the way to the goal, he was tackled hard by Angeletti and Suárez, and had the pleasure of eluding them both twice. Valussi tore his shirt, grabbed him by the arm, and kicked, and hefty Ibáñez blocked his path when he was running full tilt. But Atilio was unstoppable. The ball was part of his body and his body was a tornado, knocking over players as if they were rag dolls, until at last Atilio let the ball go with a terrifying smash that nearly burst the net.

The air smelled of gunpowder. Boca players surrounded the referee, demanding he disallow the goal because of the fouls they had committed. Since he paid them no heed, the players left the field, indignant.

the perfect kiss would like to be unique

QUITE A FEW Argentines swear, hand over heart, that Enrique García was the one. García, *El Chueco*, played left wing for Racing. Just as many Uruguayans swear, fingers crossed on their lips, that it was Pedro Lago, *El Mulero*, striker for Peñarol. It was one or the other, or perhaps both.

Half a century ago, or a little more, Lago or García scored a perfect goal, one that left his adversaries paralyzed with rage or admiration. Then he plucked the ball from the back of the net and with it under his arm he retraced his path, step by step, dragging his feet. That's right, raising lots of dust, to erase his footprints so that no one could copy the play.

the machine

IN THE EARLY forties, the Argentine club River Plate had one of the best teams of all time.

"Some go in, others come out, everyone rises, everyone falls," explained Carlos Peucelle, one of the parents of this brood. The players traded places in a permanent rotation, defenders attacked, attackers defended. "On the blackboard and on the field," Peucelle liked to say, "our tactical plan is not the traditional 1-2-3-5. It's 1-10."

Even though everyone did everything on that River team, the front line was the best. Muñoz, Moreno, Pedernera, Labruna and Loustau played only eighteen games together, but they made history and they still make for conversation. These five played by ear, whistling to each other to make their way upfield and to call the ball, which followed them like a happy dog and never got lost.

People called that legendary team "The Machine" because of its precision plays. Dubious praise: these strikers had so much fun playing they'd forget to shoot at the goal. They had nothing in common with the mechanical coldness of a machine. Fans were fairer when they called them the "Knights of Anguish" because those bastards made their devotees sweat bullets before allowing them the relief of a goal.

moreno

THEY CALLED him "El Charro" because he looked like a Mexican movie star, but he was from the countryside upriver from Buenos Aires.

José Manuel Moreno, the most popular player on River's "Machine," loved to throw fakes: his pirate legs would strike out one way but go another, his bandit head would promise a shot at one goalpost and drive it at the other.

Whenever an opponent flattened him with a kick, Moreno would get up by himself and without complaint, and no matter how badly he was hurt, he would keep on playing. He was proud, a swaggerer and a scrapper who could punch out the entire enemy stands and his own as well, since though his fans adored him they had a nasty habit of insulting him every time River lost.

Lover of good music and good friends, man of the Buenos Aires night, Moreno used to meet the dawn tangled in someone's tresses or propped up on his elbows on the counter of some café.

"The tango," he'd say, "is the best way to train: you maintain a rhythm, then change it when you stride forward, you learn the profiles, you work on your waist and your legs."

On Sundays at midday, before each match, he would devour a big bowl of chicken stew and drain several bottles of red wine. Those in charge at River ordered him to give up his rowdy ways, unbecoming of a professional athlete. He did his best. For an entire week he slept at night and drank nothing but milk. Then he played the worst game of his life. When he went back to carousing, the club suspended him. His teammates went on strike in solidarity with this incorrigible Bohemian, and River had to play nine matches with replacements.

Let's hear it for partying: Moreno had one of the longest careers in the history of soccer. He played for twenty years in the first division with clubs in Argentina, Mexico, Chile, Uruguay and Colombia. In 1946, when he returned from Mexico, River's fans were so anxious to see his daring thrusts and feints that they overflowed the stadium. More devotees knocked down the fences and invaded the playing field. He scored three goals and they carried him off on their shoulders. In 1952, Nacional in Montevideo made him a juicy offer, but he chose instead to play for another Uruguayan side, Defensor, a small club that could pay him little or nothing, because he had friends there. That year, Moreno stopped Defensor's decline.

In 1961, after retiring, he became coach of Medellín in Colombia. Medellín was losing a match against Boca Juniors from Argentina, and the players couldn't make any headway toward the goal. So Moreno, who was then forty-five, got out of his street clothes, took the field and scored two goals. Medellín won.

pedernera

"THE PENALTY kick I blocked is going down in the history of Leticia," a young Argentine wrote in a letter from Colombia. His name was Ernesto Guevara and he was not yet "Che." In 1952 he was bumming around Latin America. On the banks of the Amazon, in Leticia, he coached a soccer team. Guevara called his travelling buddy "Pedernerita." He had no better way of praising him.

Adolfo Pedernera had been the fulcrum of River's "Machine". This one-man orchestra played every position, from one end of the front line to the other. From the back he would create plays, thread the ball through the eye of a needle, change the pace, launch surprise breakaways; in front he would blow goalkeepers away.

The urge to play tickled him all over. He never wanted matches to end. When night fell, stadium employees would try in vain to get him to stop practicing. They wanted to pull him away from soccer but they couldn't, because the game refused to him let go.

goal by severino

IT WAS 1943. Boca Juniors was playing River Plate in Argentina's soccer classic.

Boca was down by a goal when the referee whistled a foul at the edge of the River area. Sosa took the free kick. Rather than shoot on goal, he served up a center pass looking for Severino Varela's head. The ball came down way ahead of Varela. River's rearguard had an easy play, Severino was nowhere near it. But the veteran striker took off and flew through the air, clawing past several defenders until he connected with a devastating beret-blow that vanquished the goalkeeper.

His fans called him the "phantom beret" because he would fly uninvited into the goalmouth. Severino had quite a few years' experience and plenty of recognition with the Uruguayan club Peñarol by the time he went to Buenos Aires, wearing the undefeated look of a mischievous child and a white beret stuck on his skull.

With Boca he sparkled. Still, every Sunday at nightfall after the game, Severino would take the boat back to Montevideo, to his barrio, his friends, and his job at the factory.

bombs

WHILE WAR tormented the world, Rio de Janeiro's dailies announced a London-style bombing on the playing field of the club Bangú. In the middle of 1943, a match was to be played against São Cristovão, and Bangú's fans planned to send four thousand fireworks aloft, the largest bombardment in the history of soccer.

When the Bangú players took the field and the gunpowder thunder and lightning began, São Cristovão's coach locked his players in the dressing room and stuck cotton in their ears. As long as the fireworks lasted, and they lasted a long time, the dressing room floor shook, the walls shook and the players shook too, all of them huddled with their heads in their hands, teeth clenched, eyes screwed shut, convinced that the World War had come home. They were still shaking when they stepped onto the field. Those who weren't epileptic must have had malaria. The sky was black with smoke. Bangú creamed them.

A short while later, there was to be a game between the Rio de Janeiro and São Paulo teams. Once again, war clouds threatened and the dailies predicted another Pearl Harbor, a siege of Leningrad and other cataclysms. The Paulistas knew that the loudest bang ever heard awaited them in Rio. Then the São Paulo coach had a brainwave: instead of hiding in the dressing room, his players would take the field at the same time as the Cariocas. That way instead of scaring them, the bombardment would be a greeting.

And that's what happened, only São Paulo lost anyway, 6-1.

the man who turned iron into wind

EDUARDO CHILLIDA tended goal for Real Sociedad in the Basque city of San Sebastián. Tall and skinny, he had a style of blocking shots that was his very own, and both Barcelona and Real Madrid had their eyes on him. The experts were predicting the boy would succeed Zamora.

But destiny had other plans. In 1943, a rival striker, appropriately named Sañudo, which means enraged, smashed Chillida's meniscus and everything else. After five operations on his knee, Chillida bid goodbye to soccer and saw no alternative but to become a sculptor.

Thus was born one of the greatest artists of the century. Chillida works with materials so heavy they sink into the earth, but his powerful hands toss iron and reinforced concrete into the air where they discover other spaces and create new dimensions on the fly. He used to do the same thing with his body.

contact therapy

ENRIQUE PICHON-REVIÈRE spent his entire life piercing the mysteries of human sadness and helping to crack our cages of silence.

In soccer he found an effective ally. Back in the forties, Pichon-Rivière organized a team among his patients at the

insane asylum. These locos were unbeatable on the fields of
the Argentine littoral, and playing was their best therapy.

"Team strategy is my priority," said the psychiatrist, who
was also the team's coach and top scorer.

Half a century later, we urban beings are all more or less
crazy, even though due to space limitations nearly all of us
live outside the asylum. Evicted by cars, trapped by violence,
condemned to isolation, we live packed in ever closer to one
another and feel ever more alone, with ever fewer meeting
places and ever less time to meet.

In soccer, as in everything else, consumers are far more
numerous than producers. Asphalt covers the empty lots
where people used to pick up a game, and work devours our
leisure time. Most people don't play, they just watch others
play on television or from stands that lie ever farther from the
field. Like carnival, soccer has become a mass spectator sport.
But just like the carnival spectators who start dancing in the
streets, in soccer there are always a few admiring fans who
kick the ball every so often out of sheer joy. And not only children. For better or for worse, though the fields are as far away
as could be, friends from the neighborhood or workmates
from the factory, the office or the faculty still get together to
play for fun until they collapse exhausted, and then winners
and losers go off together to drink and smoke and share a good
meal, pleasures denied the professional athlete.

Sometimes women take part, too, and score their own
goals, though in general the macho tradition keeps them
exiled from these fiestas of communication.

goal by martino

IT WAS 1946. The Uruguayan club Nacional was beating San Lorenzo from Argentina, so they closed up their defensive lines to meet the threat from René Pontoni and Rinaldo Martino, players who were known for making the ball speak and who had the unfortunate habit of scoring.

Martino got to the edge of Nacional's area. There he retained the ball and caressed it as if he had all the time in the world. Suddenly Pontoni crossed like lightning toward the right corner. Martino paused, raised his head, looked at him. Then the Nacional defenders all jumped on Pontoni, and while the greyhounds pursued the rabbit, Martino entered the box like a parrot into his cage, eluded the remaining fullback, shot and scored.

The goal was Martino's but it also belonged to Pontoni, who knew how to confound the enemy.

goal by heleno

IT WAS 1947. Botafogo against Flamengo in Rio de Janeiro. Botafogo striker Heleno de Freitas scored a chest goal.

Heleno had his back to the net. The ball flew down from above. He trapped it with his chest and whipped around without letting it fall. His body arched, the ball still resting on his chest, he surveyed the scene. Between him and the goal stood a multitude. There were more people in Flamengo's area than in all Brazil. If the ball hit the ground he was lost. So Heleno started walking and calmly crossed the enemy lines with his body curved back and the ball on his chest. No one could knock it off him without committing a foul, and he was in the goal area. When Heleno reached the goalmouth, he straightened up. The ball slid to his feet and he scored.

Heleno de Freitas was clearly a gypsy. He had Rudolph Valentino's face and the temper of a mad dog. On the playing field, he sparkled.

One night at the casino, he lost all his money. Another night, who knows where, he lost all his desire to live. And on his last night, delirious in a hospice, he died.

the 1950 world cup

COLOR TELEVISION was being born, computers were doing a thousand operations a second, Marilyn Monroe was making her Hollywood debut. A movie by Buñuel, "Los Olvidados," was capturing Cannes. Fangio's automobile was winning in France. Bertrand Russell was winning the Nobel. Neruda was publishing his *Canto General*, while Onetti and Octavio

Paz were bringing out the first editions of *A Brief Life* and *The Labyrinth of Solitude.*

Albizu Campos, who had fought long and hard for Puerto Rico's independence, was being sentenced to seventy-nine years in prison in the United States. An informer squealed on Salvatore Giuliano, the legendary bandit of southern Italy, and he lay dying, riddled by police bullets. In China, Mao's government was taking its first steps by outlawing polygamy and the sale of children. Wrapped in the flag of the United Nations, U.S. troops were invading the Korean peninsula by fire and sword, while soccer players were landing in Rio de Janeiro to vie for the fourth Rimet Cup after the long hiatus of the World War.

Taking part in the Brazilian tournament in 1950 were seven countries from the Americas and six from a Europe recently risen from the ashes. FIFA would not let Germany play. For the first time, England joined in the World Cup. Until then, the English had considered such skirmishes beneath them. The British side was defeated by the United States, believe it or not, and the goal that put the Americans over the top wasn't the work of General George Washington but of a black Haitian center forward named Larry Gaetjens.

Brazil and Uruguay waged the final in Maracaná, the home team's new stadium, the largest in the world. Brazil was a sure winner, the final was going to be a party. Before the match began, the Brazilian players, who had crushed all comers with goal after goal, were given gold watches with "For the World Champions" inscribed on the back. The front pages of the papers had been printed up in advance, the immense carnival float that would lead the victory parade was all set to go, half a million T-shirts with slogans celebrating the inevitable victory had already been sold.

When the Brazilian Friaça scored the first goal, the thunder of two hundred thousand voices and loads of firecrackers shook the monumental stadium. But then Schiaffino rammed in the equalizer and a shot from the wing by Ghiggia gave Uruguay the championship with a 2-1 victory. When Ghiggia scored, the silence in Maracaná was deafening, the most raucous silence in the history of soccer, and Ary Barroso, the musician and composer of *Acuarela do Brasil*, who was commenting for the entire country, swore off broadcasting for good.

After the final whistle, Brazilian commentators called the defeat, "the worst tragedy in Brazil's history." Jules Rimet wandered about the field like a lost soul, hugging the cup that bore his name: "I found myself alone with the cup in my arms and not knowing what to do. I finally found Uruguay's captain, Obdulio Varela, and I gave it to him practically without letting anyone else see. I held out my hand without saying a word."

In his pocket, Rimet had a speech he had written to congratulate the victorious Brazilians.

Uruguay had won cleanly: they committed eleven fouls to the Brazilians' twenty-one.

Third place went to Sweden. Fourth to Spain. Brazil's Ademir led the list of scorers with nine goals, followed by the Uruguayan Schiaffino with six and the Spaniard Zarra with five.

obdulio

I WAS A little kid and a soccer fan, and like every other Uruguayan I was glued to the radio in 1950, listening to the World Cup final. When the voice of Carlos Solé broadcast the melancholy news of Brazil's first goal, my heart sank to the floor. Then I turned to my most powerful friend. I promised God a heap of sacrifices if He would appear in Maracaná and turn the game around.

I never managed to remember my many promises, so I couldn't keep them. Besides, although Uruguay's victory before the largest crowd ever assembled for a soccer match was certainly a miracle, it was the work of a flesh-and-bone mortal named Obdulio Varela. Obdulio cooled the game down when the steamroller came at us, and then he carried the entire team on his shoulders. By sheer courage he fought against all the odds.

At the end of the day, reporters surrounded the hero. Obdulio didn't stick out his chest or boast about being the best. "It was one of those things," he murmured shaking his head. And when they wanted to take his picture, he turned his back.

He spent that night drinking beer in one Rio bar after another, his arm around defeated fans. The Brazilians cried. No one recognized him. The next day he dodged the crowd in the Montevideo airport where his name hung in lights. In the midst of all the euphoria he slipped away, dressed like Humphrey Bogart, in a raincoat with the lapels turned up and a fedora pulled down to his nose.

The top brass of Uruguayan soccer rewarded themselves with gold medals. They gave the players silver medals and some money. Obdulio's prize money was enough to buy a 1931 Ford. It was stolen a week later.

barbosa

WHEN IT was time to select the best goalkeeper of the '50 World Cup, journalists voted unanimously for the Brazilian Moacyr Barbosa. Without a doubt, Barbosa was the best keeper in the country, a man with rubber legs whose calm self-assurance filled the entire team with confidence, and who continued to be the best until he retired years later when he was in his forties. Over so many years of play, who knows how many goals Barbosa blocked, and he never hurt a single striker.

But in that final game in 1950, the Uruguayan attacker Ghiggia surprised him with a bull's-eye from the right wing. Barbosa had come forward. He leapt back and his fingers grazed the ball as he fell. He got up convinced that he had knocked the shot away and found the ball in the back of the net. That was the goal that left Maracaná Stadium dumbstruck and crowned Uruguay as champions.

Years went by and Barbosa was never forgiven. In 1993, during the qualifiers for the World Cup in the United States, he wanted to encourage the Brazilian players. He went to visit them at their training camp but the authorities wouldn't let him in. By then he was dependent on the generosity of his sister-in-law, living in her home with nothing but a miserable pension. Barbosa commented: "In Brazil, the most you can get for any crime is thirty years. For forty-three years I've been paying for a crime I did not commit."

goal by zarra

IT WAS at the World Cup in 1950. Spain was all over England, who only managed to shoot from afar.

Gaínza, on the wing, gobbled up the left side of the field, left half the defense sprawled on the ground and lobbed a cross towards the English goal. Ramsey, the fullback, was turned around, his back to the ball, yet he managed to graze it. Then Zarra stampeded in and rammed it home off the left post.

Telmo Zarra, leading scorer in six Spanish championships, had inherited the devotion formerly bestowed on Manolete, the bullfighter. He played on three legs, the third being his devastating head. His best-known goals were headers. In 1950 Zarra didn't score that winning goal with his head, but he certainly used it to celebrate loudly, while squeezing in his hands the little medal of the Immaculate Virgin which hung on his chest.

Top Spanish soccer official Armando Muñoz Calero, who had taken part in the Nazi invasion of Russia, sent a radio message to Generalísimo Franco: "Excellency: we have vanquished the perfidious Albion." Thus Spain finally got even with England for the defeat of the Invincible Armada in the waters of the English Channel in 1588.

Muñoz Calero dedicated the match "to the greatest Caudillo in the world." He didn't dedicate the next one to anyone. Spain faced Brazil and had to eat six goals.

goal by zizinho

AGAIN, IT was at the World Cup in 1950. In the match against Yugoslavia, Brazil's midfielder Zizinho scored a double goal.

This lord of soccer grace scored a clean goal and the referee disallowed it unfairly. So Zizinho repeated it step by step. He entered the box at the same spot, dribbled around the same Yugoslav defender with the same delicacy, slipping by on the left as before, and drove the ball in at exactly the same angle. Then he kicked the ball angrily several times against the net.

The referee understood that Zizinho was capable of repeating that goal ten more times, and had no choice but to allow it.

the fun-lovers

JULIO PÉREZ, one of the Uruguayan champions from 1950, used to cheer me up when I was a child. They called him "Pataloca," which means "Crazy Leg," because he could take himself apart in the air and leave his adversaries rubbing their eyes. They couldn't believe that his legs could fly one way while his body headed off in precisely the opposite direction. After eluding several opponents with such bodily taunts, he would back up and repeat the manoeuver. In the stands we loved to cheer this party animal of the playing field, and thanks to him we unleashed our laughter and everything else that was tied down.

Several years later I had the good luck to see the Brazilian Garrincha play, and he too had fun cracking jokes with his legs. Sometimes, when he was just at the point of climax, he'd back up, to prolong the pleasure.

the 1954 world cup

GELOSOMINA AND Zampanó sprouted from Fellini's magic hand and were clowning around leisurely in "La Strada," while Fangio surged ahead to become the world's car-racing champion for the second time. Jonas Salk was concocting a vaccine against polio. In the Pacific the first hydrogen bomb was going off. In Vietnam, General Giap was knocking out the French army in the decisive battle of Dien Bien Phu. In Algeria, another French colony, the war of independence was just beginning.

General Stroessner was being elected president of Paraguay in a close contest against himself. In Brazil, the noose tied by businessmen and brass, money and guns, was tightening around President Getulio Vargas and soon he would burst his heart with a bullet. U.S. planes were bombing Guatemala with the blessing of the OAS, and an army invented by that northern power was invading, killing and winning. While in Switzerland, the national anthems of sixteen countries were being sung to inaugurate the fifth World Cup, in Guatemala the victors were singing the United States anthem and celebrating the fall of President Arbenz, whose Marxist-Leninist ideology had been laid bare when he touched the lands of the United Fruit Company.

Taking part in the '54 World Cup were eleven teams from Europe and three from the Americas, plus Turkey and South Korea. Brazil unveiled its yellow jersey with the green collar to replace the white uniform that had brought them bad luck at Maracaná. But that canary color didn't help at first: in a violent match Brazil was defeated by Hungary and didn't even make the semi-finals. The Brazilian delegation complained to FIFA about the British referee, who acted "at the service of international communism against Western Christian civilization."

Hungary was the easy favorite to win this Cup. The steamroller combination of Puskas, Kocsis and Hidegkuti had gone four years undefeated, and shortly before the World Cup they crushed England 7-1. But it was no walkover. After the tough encounter with Brazil, the Hungarians gave their all against Uruguay. Hungary and Uruguay played to the death, neither giving any quarter, each wearing each other down, until at last two goals by Kocsis decided the game.

The final pitted Hungary against Germany, whom they had already walloped 8-3 at the beginning of the tournament when the captain Puskas was sidelined with an injury. In the final Puskas reappeared, barely scraping by on one leg, to lead a brilliant but exhausted team. Hungary was ahead 2-0, but ended up losing 3-2, and Germany won its first world title. Austria came in third, Uruguay fourth.

Kocsis the Hungarian was the leading scorer with eleven goals, followed by the German Morlock with eight and the Austrian Probst with six. Of Kocsis's eleven goals, the most incredible was against Brazil. Kocsis took off like an airplane, flew through the air and headed the ball into the corner of the goal.

goal by rahn

IT WAS at the World Cup in 1954. Hungary, the favorite, was playing Germany in the final.

With six minutes left in a game tied 2-2, the robust German forward Helmut Rahn trapped a rebound from the

Hungarian defense in the semi-circle. Rahn evaded Lantos and fired a blast with his left, just inside the right post of the goal defended by Grosics.

Heribert Zimmerman, Germany's most popular commentator, announced that goal with a passion worthy of a South American: "Toooooooooorrrrrrrrrr!!!"

It was the first World Cup that Germany had been allowed to play in since the war, and Germans felt they had the right to exist again. Zimmerman's cry became a symbol of national resurrection. Years later, that historic goal could be heard on the soundtrack of Fassbinder's film, "The Marriage of María Braun," which recounts the misadventures of a woman who can't find her way out of the ruins.

walking advertisements

IN THE mid-fifties, Peñarol signed the first contract for shirt-ads. Ten players took the field with a company name displayed on their chests. Obdulio Varela, however, stuck with his old shirt. He explained: "They used to drag us blacks around by rings in our noses. Those days are gone."

Today, every soccer player is a playing advertisement.

In 1989 Carlos Menem played a friendly game wearing the shirt of the Argentine national team, along with Maradona and the rest. On television it was hard to tell if he was the president of Argentina or of Renault, whose enormous logo he wore on his chest.

In the '94 World Cup the logos of Adidas or Umbro were more visible on players' shirts than any national symbol. The Mercedes Benz star shines alongside the federal eagle on Germany's training uniform. That same star illuminates the clothes of VfB Stuttgart. Bayern Munich, in contrast, prefers Opel cars. The packaging firm TetraPak sponsors Eintracht Frankfurt. Borussia Dortmund's players promote Continentale insurance policies, and Borussia Mönchengladbach's promote Diebels beer. The teams named for Bayer in Leverkusen and Uerdingen advertise its products, talcid and larylin, on their shirts.

The advertising on a player's chest is more important than the number on his back. In 1993 the Argentine club Racing, having no sponsor, published a desperate ad in the daily *Clarín*: "*Sponsor* wanted..." Advertising also outweighs the clean living the sport is supposed to promote. That same year, 1993, while fights in the stands in Chile reached such alarming proportions that the sale of alcohol during games was banned, most of Chile's first division teams were promoting beer or pisco on their shirts.

Speaking of clean living, a few years have gone by since the Pope performed a miracle and turned the Holy Spirit into a bank. Now the Italian club Lazio has it for a sponsor: "Banco di Santo Spirito," proclaim their shirts, as if each player were one of God's tellers.

At the end of the second quarter of 1992, the Italian company Motta took stock of its accounts. Its logo, worn proudly

on the chests of Milan's players, had been seen 2,250 times in
newspaper photos and featured for six hours on television.
Motta paid Milan four and a half million dollars; its sales of
cakes and other treats increased by $15 million over that peri-
od. Another Italian firm, Parmalat, which sells dairy products
in forty countries, had a golden year in 1993. Its team, Parma,
won the European Cup-Winners Cup for the first time, and in
South America three teams that sport its logo on their shirts,
Palmeiras, Boca and Peñarol, won championships. Clambering
over eighteen competitors, Parmalat took the Brazilian market by storm and gained a foothold among consumers in
Argentina and Uruguay—all with a helping hand from soccer.
What's more, along the way Parmalat bought several South
American teams, thus acquiring not only shirts but legs as
well. For ten million dollars, the company bought Edilson,
Mazinho, Edmundo, Cléber and Zinho, all of whom played or
once played for the Brazilian national team, as well as the
other seven players at the club Palmeiras. Anyone interested
in acquiring them should write to the company's head office in
Parma, Italy.

Ever since television started showing players up close,
the entire uniform, from head to toe, has turned into a billboard. When a star takes his time tying his shoes, it's not
slow fingers but pocketbook smarts: he's showing off the
Adidas, Nike or Reebok logo on his feet. Even back in the '36
Olympics organized by Hitler, the winning athletes featured
Adidas's three stripes on their shoes. In the '90 World Cup
final between Germany and Argentina, Adidas's stripes were
everywhere, including the ball and every strip of clothing

worn by the players, the referee and the linesmen. Two English journalists, Simpson and Jennings, reported that only the referee's whistle didn't belong to Adidas.

goal by di stéfano

IT WAS 1957. Spain was playing Belgium.

Miguel caught the Belgian defense sleeping, penetrated on the right and volleyed a cross-kick to the center. Di Stéfano leapt forward, diving full-length, and scored with a backheel from the air.

Alfredo Di Stéfano, the Argentine star who became a Spaniard, had a habit of scoring goals like that. Any open net was an unforgivable crime meriting immediate punishment, and he carried out the sentence by stabbing at it like a mischievous elf.

di stéfano

THE ENTIRE playing field fit inside his shoes. From his feet it sprouted and grew. Alfredo Di Stéfano ran and re-ran the field from net to net. He would change flanks and change rhythm with the ball, from a lazy trot to an unstoppable cyclone; without the ball he'd evade his marker to gain open space, seeking air whenever a play would get choked off.

He never stood still. Holding his head high, he could see the entire playing field and cross it at a gallop to pry open the defense and launch the attack. He was there at the beginning, the during and the end of every scoring play, and he scored goals of all colors:

Watch out, watch out,
here comes the arrow
faster than all get out.

The crowd would carry him off on their shoulders.

Di Stéfano was the engine behind three teams that amazed the world in the forties: River Plate, where he took Pedernera's place; Millonarios from Bogotá, where he sparkled alongside Pedernera; and Real Madrid, where he was Spain's leading scorer five years in a row. In 1991, years after he retired, the magazine *France Football* bestowed on this Buenos Aires boy the title of "best European player of all time."

goal by garrincha

IT WAS in Italy in 1958. Brazil's national team was playing Fiorentina on the way to the World Cup in Sweden.

Garrincha invaded the penalty area, left one defender sitting on his bottom, shook off another, and then one more. He eluded the goalkeeper too, then found another defender on the goal line. Garrincha pretended he was going to shoot, then pretended he wasn't; he faked a kick at the near corner and the poor fellow crashed face-first into the post. By then the goalkeeper was back. Garrincha put the ball between the goalie's legs and flew into the net with it.

Afterwards, with the ball under his arm, he slowly returned to the field. He walked with his gaze lowered, Chaplin in slow motion, as if asking forgiveness for that goal which had all Florence on its feet.

the 1958 world cup

THE UNITED states launched a satellite into the high heavens: a new little moon which crossed paths with Soviet sputniks but never said hello. And while the powers were competing in the Great Beyond, in the Here and Now civil war was breaking out in Lebanon, Algeria was burning, France was catching fire and General de Gaulle was standing six feet tall above the flames and promising salvation. In Cuba, Fidel Castro's general strike against the Batista dictatorship was failing, but in Venezuela another general strike was bringing down the dictatorship of Pérez Jiménez. In Colombia, Conservatives and Liberals were at the polls to bless their deal to divvy up power after a decade of mutual extermination, while Richard Nixon was being welcomed with stones on his Latin American tour. *Deep Rivers* by José María Arguedas was being published, as were Carlos Fuentes's *Where the Air is Clear* and Idea Vilariño's *Poemas de amor.*

In Hungary, Imre Nagy was being shot along with other rebels from '56 who wanted democracy instead of bureaucracy, and dying too were the Haitian rebels who had launched an assault on the palace where Papa Doc Duvalier reigned amid sorcerers and executioners. John XXIII, John the Good, was the new Pope in Rome; Prince Charles was the future monarch of England; Barbie was the new queen of dolls. In Brazil João Havelange was conquering the throne in the industry of soccer, while in the art of soccer a seventeen-year-old kid named Pelé was being hailed king of the world.

The consecration of Pelé took place in Sweden during the sixth World Cup. Participating were twelve teams from Europe, four from the Americas and none from other latitudes. Swedes could watch at the stadium or in their homes. This was the first Cup to be televised, although it was only broadcast live in Sweden. The rest of the world saw it later.

This was also the first time that a country playing outside its own continent won. At the beginning of the '58 World

Cup the Brazilians didn't have much spark, but after the players rebelled and convinced the coach to field the team they wanted, they were unstoppable. At that point five substitutes became starters, among them an unknown teenager named Pelé, and Garrincha, who was already quite famous in Brazil and had sparkled in the previous Cup. Garrincha had been left out this time because psychological testing showed him to have a weak mind. These black second-stringers to white starters blazed with their own light in the new star team, along with another astonishing black, Didí, who organized their magic from the back.

Games and flames: the London paper *World Sports* said you had to rub your eyes to believe that it was of this world. In the semi-final against the French team of Kopa and Fontaine, the Brazilians won 5-2, and they won again 5-2 in the final against the home team. The Swedish captain, Liedholm, one of the cleanest and most elegant players in the history of soccer, converted the first goal of the match, but then Vavá, Pelé and Zagalo put the Swedes in their place under the astonished gaze of King Gustavus Adolphus. Brazil became champions without suffering a single defeat. When it was over, the victorious players gave the ball to their most devoted fan, the black masseur Américo.

France took third place and West Germany fourth. Fontaine of France led the list of scorers with a shower of thirteen goals, eight with the right leg, four with the left and one with his head, followed by Pelé and Helmut Rahn of Germany who scored six apiece.

goal by nílton

IT WAS at the World Cup in 1958. Brazil was leading Austria 1-0.

At the beginning of the second half, the key to the Brazilian defense, Nílton Santos, who was called "The Encyclopedia" for his vast knowledge of soccer, abandoned the rearguard, passed the center line, eluded a pair of opposing players and kept going. The Brazilian coach, Vicente Feola, was also running but on the other side of the touchline. Sweating buckets he screamed: "Go back! Go back!"

Nílton, unflappable, continued his race toward the enemy area. A fat and desperate Feola clutched his head but Nílton refused to pass the ball to any of the forwards. He made the play entirely on his own and it culminated in a tremendous goal.

Then a happy Feola commented, "Did you see that? Didn't I tell you? This one really knows!"

garrincha

ONE OF HIS many brothers baptized him Garrincha, the name of an ugly, useless little bird. When he started playing soccer, doctors made the sign of the cross. They predicted this misshapen survivor of hunger and polio, dumb and lame, with the brain of an infant, a spinal column like an S and both legs bowed to the same side, would never be an athlete.

There never was another right winger like him. In the '58 World Cup he was the best in his position, in '62 the best player in the championship. But throughout his many years on the field, Garrincha was more: in the entire history of soccer no one made more people happy.

When he was playing, the field became a circus ring, the ball a tame beast, the game an invitation to a party. Like a child defending his pet, Garrincha wouldn't let go of the ball, and the ball and he would perform devilish tricks that had people dying of laughter. He would jump on her, she would hop on him, she would hide, he would escape, she would chase after him. In the process, the opposing players would crash into each other, their legs twisting around until they would fall, seasick, to the ground. Garrincha did his rascal's mischief at the edge of the field, along the right touchline, far from the center: raised in the shantytown suburbs, that's where he played. He played for a club called Botafogo, which means "firelighter," and he was the botafogo who fired up the fans crazed by fire water and all things fiery. He was the one who climbed out of the training-camp window because he heard from far-off back alleys the call of a ball asking to be played with, music demanding to be danced to, a woman wanting to be kissed.

A winner? A lucky loser. And luck doesn't last. As they say in Brazil, if shit was worth anything, the poor would be born without asses.

Garrincha died a predictable death: poor, drunk and alone.

didí

THE PRESS named him best playmaker of the '58 Cup.

He was the hub of the Brazilian team. Lean body, long neck, poised statue of himself, Didí looked like an African icon standing at the center of the field. There he was lord and master. From there he would shoot his poison arrows.

He was a master of the long ball, a near goal that would become a real goal on the feet of Pelé, Garrincha or Vavá, but he also scored on his own. Shooting from afar, he used to fool goalkeepers with the "dry leaf": by giving the ball his foot's profile, she would leave the ground spinning and continue spinning on the fly, dancing about and changing direction like a dry leaf carried by the wind, until she flew between the posts precisely where the goalkeeper least expected.

Didí played unhurriedly. Pointing at the ball, he'd say: "She's the one who runs."

He knew she was alive.

didí and she

I ALWAYS felt a lot of affection for her. Because if you don't treat her with affection, she won't obey. When she'd come, I'd take charge and she'd obey. Sometimes she'd go one way and I'd say:

"Come here, child," and I'd bring her along. I'd take care of her blisters and warts and she'd always sit there, obedient as can be. I'd treat her with as much affection as I give my own wife. I had tremendous affection for her. Because she's fire. If you treat her badly, she'll break your leg. That's why I say: "Boys, come on, have some respect. This is a girl that has to be treated with a lot of love. . . " Depending on the spot where you touch her, she'll choose your fate.

(Testimony collected by Roberto Moura)

kopa

THEY CALLED him "the Napoleon of soccer" because he was short and he liked to conquer territory.

With the ball on his foot he grew taller and dominated the field. Raymond Kopa was a player of great mobility and florid feints, who drew arabesques on the grass as he danced his way toward the goal. Coaches pulled their hair out watching him have so much fun with the ball and French experts often accused him of having a South American style. But in the '58 World Cup, the press named Kopa a star and that year he won the Golden Boot for being the best player in Europe.

Soccer had pulled him out of misery. He began playing for

a team of miners. The son of Polish immigrants, Kopa spent his childhood at his father's side in the Noeux coal pits. He'd go down every night and emerge the following afternoon.

carrizo

HE SPENT a quarter of a century catching balls with magnetic hands and sowing panic in the enemy camp. Amadeo Carrizo founded a style of South American play. He was the first goal-keeper who had the audacity to leave the penalty area and lead the attack. Heightening the danger, on more than one occasion this Argentine even took the enormous risk of dribbling past opposing players. Before Carrizo, such insanity was unthinkable. Then his audacity caught on. His compatriot Gatti, the Colombian Higuita and the Paraguayan Chilavert also refused to resign themselves to the notion that the keeper is a living wall, glued to the net. They proved he can also be a living spear.

As we all know, fans delight in hating the enemy: rival players always deserve condemnation or scorn. But Argentine fans of all stripes praise Carrizo, and all but one or two agree that on that country's fields no one ever blocked shots as well as he did. Nevertheless, in 1958 when the Argentine team returned with their tails between their legs after the World Cup in Sweden, it was the idol who caught the most heat. Argentina had been beaten by Czechoslovakia 6-1, and such treason demanded a public expiation. The press pilloried him, the crowds hissed and whistled and Carrizo was crushed. Years later in his memoirs he confessed sadly: "I remember the goals they scored on me better than the shots I blocked."

shirt fervor

URUGUAYAN WRITER Paco Espínola didn't like soccer. But one afternoon in the summer of 1960, when he was scanning the radio dial for something to listen to, he chanced upon the local classic. Peñarol was routed by Nacional 4-0.

When night fell, Paco felt so depressed he decided to eat alone so as not to embitter the life of anyone else. Where did all that sadness come from? Paco was prepared to believe there was no particular reason, perhaps the sheer sorrow of being mortal. Suddenly it hit him: he was sad because Peñarol had lost. He was a Peñarol fan and hadn't known it.

How many Uruguayans were sad like him? And how many, on the other hand, were jumping with joy? Paco experienced a delayed revelation. Normally we Uruguayans *belong* to Nacional or to Peñarol from the day we are born. People say, for example, "I'm a Peñarol," or "I'm a Nacional." That's the way it's been since the beginning of the century. They say that back then the professionals of love used to attract clients by sitting in the doorways of Montevideo's bordellos wearing nothing but the shirts of Peñarol or Nacional.

For the fanatic, pleasure comes not from your own club's victory, but from the other's defeat. In 1993 a Montevideo daily interviewed a group of young men who supported themsleves carrying firewood all week and enjoyed themselves screaming for Nacional in the stadium on Sundays. One of them confessed: "For me, just the sight of a Peñarol shirt makes me sick. I want them to lose every time, even if they play against foreigners."

It's the same story in other divided cities. In 1988, in the final of the Copa América, Nacional beat Newell's, one of two clubs that share the adoration of the city of Rosario on the Argentine littoral. The fans of the other club, Rosario Central, filled the streets to celebrate the defeat of Newell's at the hands of a foreign team.

I think it was Osvaldo Soriano who told me the story of the death of a Boca Juniors fan in Buenos Aires. That fan had spent his entire life hating the club River Plate, as was entirely appropriate, but on his deathbed he asked to be wrapped in the enemy flag. That way he could celebrate with his final breath the death of "one of them."

If the fan *belongs* to a club, why not the players? Rarely will a fan accept an idol in a new venue. Changing clubs is not the same as changing jobs, although the player is indeed a professional who earns his living by his legs. Loyalty to the uniform just doesn't fit with modern soccer, but the fans still mete out punishment for the crime of desertion. In 1989, when the Brazilian player Bebeto left Flamengo for Vasco da Gama, some Flamengo fans went to Vasco da Gama games just to boo the traitor. Threats rained down on him and the most fearful sorcerer in Rio de Janeiro put a spell on him. Bebeto suffered a rosary of injuries, he simply could not play without getting hurt, and things went from bad to worse until he finally decided to move to Spain. Some years earlier, the long-time star of the Argentine club Racing, Roberto Perfumo, moved over to River Plate. His loyal fans gave him one of the longest and loudest catcalls in history: "I realized how much they loved me," Perfumo said.

Nostalgic for the faithful old days, fans also are loath to accept the calculations of profitability that often determine such decisions, now that every club has been obliged to become a factory for producing extravaganzas. When business isn't going well, red ink cries out for sacrificing some of the company's assets. The gigantic Carrefour supermarket chain in Buenos Aires built a store on the ruins of San Lorenzo's stadium. When the stadium was demolished in the middle of 1983, weeping fans carried off fistfuls of dirt in their pockets.

The club is the only identity card fans believe in. And in many cases the shirt, the anthem and the flag embody deeply felt traditions which may find expression on the playing fields but spring from the depths of community history. For Catalonians, the Barcelona team is more than a club, it is a symbol of their long struggle for national affirmation against the central power in Madrid. Since 1919, no foreigners and no other Spaniards have played for Athletic in Bilbao. A bastion of Basque pride, Athletic only takes Basque players into its ranks, and they are nearly always players from their own farm teams. During the long dictatorship of Franco, two stadiums, Nou Camp in Barcelona and San Mamés in Bilbao, were sanctuaries for outlawed nationalist sentiment. There, Catalonians and Basques could shout and sing in their own languages and wave their outlawed flags. The first time the Basque standard was raised without provoking a beating from the police was in a soccer stadium. A year after Franco's death, the players of Athletic and Real Sociedad carried the flag onto the field.

Yugoslavia's war of disintegration, which so upset the entire world, began on the soccer field before it took to the battlefield. The ancient resentment between Serbs and Croats came to the surface every time clubs from Belgrade and Zagreb faced each other. Fans revealed their deep passions and dug up flags and chants from the past to use as battle axes.

goal by puskas

IT WAS 1961. Real Madrid was playing at home against Atlético of Madrid.

No sooner had the game begun when Ferenc Puskas scored a double goal, just as Zizinho had in the '50 World

Cup. The Hungarian striker for Real Madrid executed a free kick at the edge of the box and the ball went in. But as Puskas celebrated with his arms in the air the referee went up to him. "I'm sorry," he said, "but I didn't whistle."

So Puskas shot again. He kicked with his left foot, as before, and the ball traveled exactly the same path: like a cannonball over the heads of the same players in the wall and, just like the goal that had been disallowed, it landed in the upper left corner of the net tended by Madinabeytia, who leapt as before and, as before, was unable even to graze it.

goal by sanfilippo

DEAR EDUARDO,

I've got to tell you about this. The other day I went to the Carrefour supermarket, the one built where San Lorenzo used to play. I was with my childhood hero José Sanfilippo, who was San Lorenzo's leading scorer four seasons in a row. There we were, walking among shopping carts, surrounded by pots and pans and cheeses and strings of sausages. All of a sudden, as we head for the check-out, Sanfilippo opens his arms and says: "To think that it was right here where I rammed it in on Roma with a half-volley in that match against Boca." He walks in front of a housewife pushing a cart filled to the brim with cans, steaks and vegetables, and he says: "It was the fastest goal in history."

He concentrates, as if he were waiting for a corner kick, and says to me: "I told the center-half, a young fellow, 'As soon as the game begins send me the ball in the box. Take it easy, I won't make you look bad.' I was older and this kid, Capdevilla was his name, was scared, thinking, 'What if I don't come through?'" And then Sanfilippo points to a stack of mayonnaise jars and screams: "He put it right here!" People are looking at us like we're nuts. "The ball dropped over the halfbacks, I stumbled but it rolled a bit back to there where the rice is, see?" He points to the bottom shelf, and all of a sudden he starts running like a rabbit in spite of his blue suit and shiny shoes. "I let it bounce and boom!" He swings his left leg in a tremendous kick. We all spin around to look at the check-out, where the goal sat thirty-odd years ago, and it's as if we all see the ball hit the net up high, right by the batteries and the razor blades. Sanfilippo raises his arms to celebrate. The shoppers and the check-out girls pound their hands applauding. I'm practically in tears. "El Nene" Sanfilippo scored that goal from 1962 all over again, just so I could see it.

Osvaldo Soriano

the 1962 world cup

A FEW Indian and Malaysian astrologists were predicting the end of the world, but it kept on turning, and as it turned an organization with the name of Amnesty International was born, and Algeria took its first steps of independent life after more than seven years of war against France. In Israel, the Nazi criminal Adolph Eichmann was being hanged, the miners of Asturias were on strike, and Pope John was trying to change the Church and return it to the poor. They were making the first computer disks and performing the first operations with laser beams, and Marilyn Monroe was losing her will to live.

What was the price of a country's vote? Haiti sold its franchise for fifteen million dollars, a highway, a dam and a hospital, and that's how the OAS got a majority to expel Cuba, the black sheep of Pan-Americanism. Well-informed sources in Miami announced the imminent fall of Fidel Castro, it was only a matter of hours. Seventy-five suits were launched in U.S. courts to ban the novel *Tropic of Cancer* by Henry Miller, published for the first time in an unexpurgated edition. Linus Pauling, who was about to win his second Nobel Prize, was picketing the White House to protest against nuclear testing, while Benny "Kid" Paret, an illiterate black Cuban, was dying, beaten to a pulp, in the ring at Madison Square Garden.

In Memphis, Elvis Presley announced his retirement after selling three hundred million records, but before long he changed his mind; in London a record company, Decca, refused to record the songs of a group of hairy musicians who called themselves The Beatles. Carpentier was publishing *Explosion in the Cathedral*, Gelman was publishing *Gotán*, the Argentine military were overthrowing President Frondizi, and the Brazilian painter Cándido Portinari was dying. *Primeiras estórias* by Guimaraes Rosa was in the bookstores, as were the poems that Vinícius de Moraes wrote *para viver um grande amor*. João Gilberto was crooning "One-Note Samba" in Carnegie Hall while the Brazilian team was arriving in Chile, expecting to win the seventh World Cup against five other countries from the Americas and ten from Europe.

In the '62 World Cup Di Stéfano wasn't very lucky. He was going to play for his adopted country, Spain. At thirty-six this would be his last chance. Just before the opening game, he hurt his right knee and there was no way he could play. Di Stéfano, "The Blond Arrow," one of the best players in the history of soccer, never played in a World Cup. Pelé, another all-time star, didn't get very far in Chile either: he pulled a muscle at the start and couldn't play. And one more sacred giant of soccer, the Russian Yashin, also turned into a lame duck: the best goalkeeper in the world let in four goals against Colombia, because, it seems, he bucked himself up with a few too many nips in the dressing room.

Brazil won the tournament without Pelé and under Didí's charge. Amarildo sparkled in the difficult role of filling Pelé's shoes, Djalma Santos made himself into a wall on defense and up front Garrincha was inspired and inspiring. "What planet is Garrincha from?" asked the daily *El Mercurio*, when Brazil liquidated the home team. The Chileans had beaten Italy in a match that was a pitched battle, and they also beat Switzerland and the Soviet Union. They gobbled down spaghetti, chocolate and vodka, but choked on the coffee: Brazil won 4-2.

In the final, Brazil downed Czechoslovakia 3-1 and, just as in '58, was the undefeated champion. For the very first time the World Cup final was broadcast live internationally on television, though it was in black and white and reached only a few countries.

Chile won third place, its best ranking ever, and Yugoslavia won fourth thanks to a bird named Dragoslav Sekularac whom no defender could catch.

The championship did not have a leading scorer, but several players notched up four goals: Garrincha and Vavá of Brazil, Sánchez of Chile, Jerkovic of Yugoslavia, Albert of Hungary and Ivanov of the Soviet Union.

goal by charlton

IT WAS at the '62 World Cup. England was playing Argentina.

Bobby Charlton set up the first English goal by placing the ball where Flowers could face the goalkeeper Roma alone. But the second goal was Charlton's from start to finish. Charlton, lord of the entire left side of the field, made the

Argentine defense collapse like swatted moths. He changed feet at full tilt and with his right overwhelmed the keeper with a strike from the wing.

He was a survivor. Practically all the players on his team, Manchester United, died in the twisted ruins of a burning plane. Death spared this miner's son so he could continue giving people the high nobility of his soccer.

The ball obeyed him. She travelled the field following his instructions and flew into the net before he even kicked her.

yashin

WHEN LEV YASHIN covered the goal, not a pinhole was left open. This giant with long spidery arms always dressed in black and played with a naked elegance that disdained unnecessary gestures. He liked to stop thundering blasts with a single claw-like hand that trapped and shredded any projectile, while his body remained motionless like a rock. He could deflect the ball with a glance.

He retired from soccer several times, always pursued by torrents of gratitude, and several times he returned. There was no other like him. During more than a quarter of a century, this Russian blocked over a hundred penalty shots and saved who-knows-how-many goals. When asked for his secret, he'd say the trick was to have a smoke to calm your nerves, then toss back a strong drink to tone your muscles.

goal by gento

IT WAS 1963. Real Madrid faced Pontevedra.

As soon as the referee blew the opening whistle, there was a goal by Di Stéfano. Then right at the beginning of the second half Puskas scored. From that point on the fans waited in suspense for the next goal, which would be the 2,000th for Real Madrid since it started playing in the Spanish League in 1928. Madrid fans invoked the goal by kissing their fingers while making the sign of the cross, and the enemy fans warded it off by pointing their index and little fingers at the ground.

The game turned around. Pontevedra began to dominate. When night fell and only a few minutes remained, and that goal so desired and so feared seemed lost from sight, Amancio shot a dangerous free kick: he sent the ball to Di Stéfano, who couldn't reach the pass, but Gento got it. The Madrid left winger broke free of the defenders surrounding him, shot and won. The stadium went wild.

All rival teams were on the look-out to capture Francisco

Gento, the fugitive. Sometimes they managed to put him behind bars, but he always slipped out.

seeler

A JOLLY FACE. You couldn't imagine him without a mug of foaming beer in his fist. On Germany's soccer fields he was always the shortest and the stoutest: a pudgy pink hamburger with an unsteady gait, because one foot was larger than the other. But Uwe Seeler was a flea when he jumped, a hare when he ran and a bull when he headed the ball.

In 1964 this center forward for Hamburg was chosen as the best player in Germany. He belonged to Hamburg body and soul: "I'm just another fan. This team is my home," he said. Uwe Seeler scorned numerous juicy offers to play on Europe's most powerful teams. He played in four World Cups. To shout "Uwe, Uwe," was the best way of shouting, "Germany, Germany."

matthews

IN 1965, when he was fifty years old, Stanley Matthews still caused serious outbreaks of hysteria in British soccer. There weren't enough psychiatrists to deal with all the victims, who had been perfectly normal until the moment they were bewitched by this grandfatherly tormentor of fullbacks.

Defenders would grab his shirt or his shorts, they'd get him in wrestling holds or tackle him with kicks worthy of the police blotter, but nothing stopped him because they never managed to clip his wings. Matthews was precisely that, a winger, the one who flew highest over the sidelines of England.

Queen Elizabeth was well aware of this: she made him a knight.

the 1966 world cup

The military were bathing Indonesia in blood, half a million, a million dead, who knows how many, and General Suharto was inaugurating his long dictatorship by murdering the few reds, pinks or questionables still alive. Other officers were overthrowing Nkrumah, president of Ghana and prophet of African unity, while their colleagues in Argentina were evicting President Illia by a coup.

For the first time in history a woman, Indira Gandhi, governed India. Students were toppling Ecuador's military dictatorship. The U.S. Air Force was bombing Hanoi with renewed vigor, but the American public was growing ever more convinced they should never have gone into Vietnam, let alone stayed, and should leave as soon as possible.

Truman Capote had just published *In Cold Blood.* García Márquez's *One Hundred Years of Solitude* and Lezama Lima's *Paradiso* appeared. The priest Camilo Torres was dying in battle in the mountains of Colombia, Che Guevara was riding his skinny Rocinante through Bolivia's countryside, Mao was unleashing the Cultural Revolution in China. Several atomic bombs fell on the Spanish coast at Almería, sowing panic even though they did not go off. Well-informed sources in Miami announced the imminent fall of Fidel Castro, it was only a matter of hours.

In London, with Harold Wilson chewing his pipestem and celebrating victory at the polls, young women sporting miniskirts, Carnaby Street as fashion capital and the entire world humming Beatles tunes, the eighth World Cup got underway.

This was the final World Cup for Garrincha and it was also a good-bye party for Mexican goalkeeper Antonio Carbajal, the only man who played in the tournament five times.

Sixteen teams took part: ten from Europe, five from the Americas and, strange as it seems, North Korea. Astonishingly, the Koreans eliminated Italy with a goal by Pak, a dentist from the city of Pyongyang who played soccer in his spare time. On the Italian squad were no less than Gianni Rivera and Sandro Mazzola. Pier Paolo Pasolini used to say they played soccer in lucid prose interspersed with sparkling verse, but that dentist left them speechless.

For the first time the entire championship was broadcast live by satellite, and though in black and white, the whole world could watch the show put on by the referees. In the previous World Cup, European referees officiated at twenty-six matches; in this one, they ran twenty-four out of thirty-two. A German referee gave England the match against Argentina, while an English referee gave Germany the match against Uruguay. Brazil had no better luck: Pelé was hunted down and kicked with impunity by Bulgaria and Portugal, who knocked Brazil out of the championship.

Queen Elizabeth attended the final. She didn't scream when people scored, rather she applauded discreetly. The World Cup came down to the England of Bobby Charlton, a man of fearful drive and marksmanship, and the Germany of Beckenbauer, who had just begun his career and was already playing with hat, gloves and cane. Someone had stolen the Rimet Cup, but a dog named Pickles found it in a London garden, and the trophy reached the winner's hands in time. England won 4–2. Portugal came in third. In fourth place, the Soviet Union. Queen Elizabeth gave Alf Ramsey, the coach of the winning team, a title of nobility, and Pickles became a national hero.

The '66 World Cup was usurped by defensive tactics. Every team used the sweeper system with an extra defender by the goal line behind the fullbacks. Even so, Eusebio,

Portugal's African artilleryman, managed to pierce those impenetrable rearguard walls nine times. Behind him on the list of leading scorers was Haller of Germany, with six.

greaves

IN A WESTERN he would have been the fastest shot. On the soccer field he scored a hundred goals before he was twenty, and by the time he was twenty-five they still hadn't invented a lightning rod that could ground him. Rather than run, he would explode: Jimmy Greaves pushed off so fast the referees used to call him off-side by mistake, because they couldn't figure out where his sudden stabs and bull's-eye shots came from. They'd see him land, but they never saw him take off.

"I want to score so badly," he'd say, "it hurts."

Greaves had no luck at the '66 World Cup. He didn't score a single goal, and an attack of jaundice made him sit out the final.

goal by beckenbauer

IT WAS at the '66 World Cup. Germany was playing Switzerland.

Uwe Seeler launched the attack along with Franz Beckenbauer, the two of them like Sancho Panza and Don Quijote, fired onto the field by an invisible trigger, back and forth, yours and mine. Once the entire Swiss defense was left useless as a deaf ear, Beckenbauer faced the goalie, Elsener, who leapt to his left. Beckenbauer pivoted at full tilt, shot to the right and in it went.

Beckenbauer was twenty and that was his first goal in a World Cup. After '66 he took part in four more, as player or coach, and never finished below third place. Twice he embraced the World Cup: playing in '74 and coaching in '90. Bucking the trend towards a soccer of sheer Panzer-style strength, he proved that elegance can be more powerful than a tank and delicacy more penetrating than a howitzer.

This emperor of the midfield, known as "The Kaiser," was born in a working-class section of Munich. And he nobly commanded both the attack and the defense: in the back nothing escaped him, not one ball, not a fly, not a mosquito could get through; and when he attacked he was like fire.

eusebio

HE WAS BORN to shine shoes, sell peanuts or pick pockets. As a child they called him "Ninguém": no one, nobody. Son of a widowed mother, he played soccer from dawn to dusk with his many brothers in the empty lots of the shantytowns.

He set foot on the field running as only someone with the police or poverty nipping at his heels can run. That's how he became champion of Europe at the age of twenty, sprinting in zig zags. They called him "The Panther."

In the '66 World Cup his attacks left adversaries scattered on the ground, and his goals from impossible angles set off never-ending ovations.

Portugal's best player ever was an African from Mozambique. Eusebio: long legs, dangling arms, sad eyes.

curse of the three posts

THIS KEEPER had a face chiseled with an ax and pocked by smallpox. His huge, gnarled hands bolted and padlocked the net, and his feet shot off cannonballs. Of all the Brazilian goalkeepers I've ever seen, Manga is the one I remember most. Once in Montevideo I saw him score a goal from net to net: Manga kicked from his goal and the ball went into the opponents' goal without any other player touching it. He was playing for the Uruguayan club Nacional as a penance. He had no choice but to leave Brazil. The Brazilian team went home shamefaced from the '66 World Cup, having suffered an ignominious defeat, and Manga was the scapegoat for their national disgrace. He only played in one match. He made a mistake, got drawn out, and as bad luck would have it Portugal scored a goal on the empty net. That unfortunate moment was such a scandal that for a long time errors by goalkeepers came to be known as *mangueiradas*.

Something like that happened in the '58 World Cup, when the keeper Amadeo Carrizo paid the price for Argentina's defeat. And before that, in '50, when Moacyr Barbosa was the whipping boy for Brazil's loss in the final at Maracaná.

In the '90 World Cup Cameroon unseated Colombia after winning a brilliant match against Germany. The African team's winning goal came on a foolish mistake by keeper René Higuita, who took the ball up to midfield and lost it there. The same people who like to cheer such audacity when it turns out well wanted to eat Higuita alive when he got back to Colombia.

In 1993 the Colombian team, without Higuita, crushed Argentina 5-0 in Buenos Aires. Such a humiliation cried out for someone to blame, and the guilty party had to be—who else?—the goalkeeper. Sergio Goycoechea paid for all the broken dishes. The Argentine team had been undefeated in thirty matches, and in each one Goycoechea was the key to their success. But after Colombia's goalfest the miracle penalty-blocker not only lost his nickname, Saint Goyco, he also lost his spot on the team. More than one fan recommended suicide.

peñarol's glory years

IN 1966 the champions of the Americas and Europe, Peñarol and Real Madrid, faced each other twice. With fancy dribbling, beautiful plays, and barely any sweat on their shirts, Peñarol won both matches 2-0.

In the sixties, Peñarol inherited the scepter from Real Madrid, the greatest team of the previous decade. Peñarol won the Inter-Continental Cup twice in those years and was champion of the Americas three times.

When the best squad in the world took the field, they said to the opposing players: "Did you bring another ball? This one belongs to us."

The ball was forbidden entry to Mazurkiewicz's net, in the midfield she obeyed the orders of "Tito" Gonçalves, and up front she buzzed on the feet of Spencer and Joya. At "Pepe" Sasía's command, she would pierce the goal. But she had fun too, especially when Pedro Rocha would swing her back and forth.

goal by rocha

IT WAS 1969. Peñarol was playing Estudiantes from La Plata.

Rocha was at the center of the field, marked by two players, with his back to the enemy area, when he got the ball from Matosas. He put it to sleep on his right foot, spun around with the ball still there, slipped it behind his other foot and escaped his markers, Echecopar and Taverna. He made three quick dashes, left the ball to Spencer and continued running. The return pass came in high in the semi-circle. He trapped it with his chest, broke free of Madero and Spadaro and volleyed a shot before it hit the ground. The goalkeeper, Flores, didn't even see it.

Pedro Rocha slid along like a snake in the grass. He played joyfully and his joy was infectious: the joy of the play, the joy of the goal. He did whatever he wanted with the ball, and she believed every bit of it.

my poor beloved mother

AT THE END of the sixties, the poet Jorge Enrique Adoum returned to Ecuador after a long absence. As soon as he arrived, he performed an obligatory ritual in the city of Quito: he went to the stadium to see the Aucas play. It was an important match and the stands were packed.

Before the kick-off, there was a minute of silence for the mother of the referee who had died that morning. Everyone stood, everyone was silent. Then someone made a speech praising the dedication of this exemplary sportsman who was going to officiate, performing his duty even in the most difficult of circumstances. At the center of the field, his head bowed, the man in black acknowledged the sustained applause of the crowd. Adoum blinked, he pinched himself, he couldn't believe it. What country was he in? So much had changed. Before, people's only concern for the referee was to call him a son of a bitch.

And the match began. At fifteen minutes Aucas scored and the stadium exploded. But the referee disallowed the goal due to an off-side, and the thoughts of the crowd turned immediately to his deceased mater: "Orphan of a bitch!" roared the stands.

tears don't flow from a handkerchief

SOCCER, METAPHOR for war, at times turns into real war. Then "sudden death" is no longer just a dramatic way of deciding a tied match. These days, soccer fanaticism has come to occupy the place formerly reserved for religious fervor, patriotic ardor and political passion. As often occurs with religion, patriotism and politics, soccer can bring tensions to a boil, and many horrors are committed in its name.

Some believe men possessed by the demon of the ball foam at the mouth, and frankly that image presents a fairly accurate picture of the frenzied fan. But even the most indignant of critics would concede that in most cases violence doesn't originate in soccer, any more than tears flow from a handkerchief.

In 1969, war broke out between Honduras and El Salvador, two small and very poor Central American countries that for over a century had been accumulating reasons to distrust each other. Each had always served as the magical explanation for the other's problems. Hondurans don't have work? Because Salvadorans come and take their jobs. Salvadorans are hungry? Because Hondurans mistreat them. Each country believed their neighbor was the enemy, and the incessant military dictatorships of each did all they could to perpetuate the error.

This war was called the Soccer War because the sparks that set off the conflagration were struck in the stadiums of Tegucigalpa and San Salvador. The trouble began during the play-offs for the '70 World Cup. There were tussles, a few injuries, several deaths. A week later, the two countries broke off relations. Honduras expelled a hundred thousand Salvadoran peasants who had always worked in that country's plantings and harvests; Salvadoran tanks crossed the border.

The war lasted a week and killed four thousand people. The two governments, dictatorships forged at a U.S. factory called the School of the Americas, fanned the fires of mutual hatred. In Tegucigalpa the slogan was, "Honduran don't sit still, grab a stick and a Salvadoran kill." In San Salvador: "Teach those barbarians a lesson." The lords of land and war didn't lose a drop of blood, while two barefoot peoples avenged their identical misfortunes by killing each other with patriotic fervor.

goal by pelé

IT WAS in 1969. Santos was playing Vasco da Gama in Maracaná Stadium.

Pelé crossed the field in a flash, evading his opponents without ever touching the ground, and when he was about to enter the goal with the ball he was tripped.

The referee whistled a penalty. Pelé didn't want to take it. A hundred thousand people forced him to, screaming out his name.

Pelé had scored many goals in Maracaná. Prodigious goals, like the one in 1961 against Fluminense when he dribbled past seven defenders and the goalie. But this penalty was different: people felt there was something sacred about it. That's why the noisiest crowd in the world fell silent. The clamor disappeared as if obeying an order: no one spoke, no one breathed. All of a sudden the stands seemed empty and so did the field. Pelé and the goalie, Andrada, were alone. By themselves, they waited. Pelé stood by the ball resting on the penalty spot. Twelve paces beyond stood Andrada, hunched over at the ready, between the two posts.

The goalkeeper managed to graze the ball, but Pelé nailed it to the net. It was his thousandth goal. No other player in the history of professional soccer had ever scored a thousand goals.

Then the multitude came back to life and jumped like a child overjoyed, lighting up the night.

pelé

A HUNDRED songs name him. At seventeen he was champion of the world and king of soccer. Before he was twenty the government of Brazil named him a "national treasure" that could not be exported. He won three world championships with the Brazilian team and two with the club Santos. After his thousandth goal, he kept on counting. He played more than thirteen hundred matches in eighty countries, one game after another at a punishing rate, and he scored nearly thirteen hundred goals. Once he held up a war: Nigeria and Biafra declared a truce to see him play.

To see him play was worth a truce and a lot more. When Pelé ran hard he cut right through his opponents like a hot knife through butter. When he stopped, his opponents got lost in the labyrinths his legs embroidered. When he jumped, he climbed into the air as if there were a staircase. When he executed a free kick, his opponents in the wall wanted to turn around to face the net, so as not to miss the goal.

He was born in a poor home in a far-off village, and he reached the summit of power and fortune where blacks were not allowed. Off the field he never gave a minute of his time and a coin never fell from his pocket. But those of us who were lucky enough to see him play received alms of an extraordinary beauty: moments so worthy of immortality that they make us believe immortality exists.

like Michael Jordan

the 1970 world cup

IN RAGUE, cinema puppet master Jiri Trnka was dying; so was Bertrand Russell in London, after nearly a century of very lively living. After only twenty years the poet Rugama was cut down in Managua, fighting alone against one of the Somoza dictatorship's battalions. The world lost its music: the Beatles broke up, due to an overdose of success, and due to an overdose of drugs guitarist Jimi Hendrix and singer Janis Joplin took their leave.

A hurricane was ripping through Pakistan while an earthquake erased fifteen cities from the Peruvian Andes. In Washington no one believed in the Vietnam War anymore, but the war kept dragging on with the death toll reaching a million, according to the Pentagon, and the generals fleeing forwards by invading Cambodia. After losing in three previous attempts, Allende was launching his campaign for the presidency of Chile, promising milk for every child and to nationalize the nation's copper. Well-informed sources in Miami announced the imminent fall of Fidel Castro, it was only a matter of hours. For the first time in history, the Vatican was on strike. While employees of the Holy Father in Rome crossed their arms, in Mexico, players from sixteen countries moved their legs to begin the ninth World Cup.

Nine teams from Europe, five from the Americas, plus Israel and Morocco took part. In the first match, the referee raised the yellow card for the first time. The yellow card, sign of warning, and the red card, sign of expulsion, were not the only novelties at the Mexico World Cup. The rules allowed for two substitutions during the course of each game. Before then, only the goalkeeper could be replaced in case of injury and it was never very hard to reduce the adversary's number with a few well placed kicks.

Images of the '70 World Cup: the impression left by Beckenbauer as he battled to the final minute with one arm in a sling; the fervor of Tostão, fresh from an eye operation and managing a sure-footed performance in every game; the aerobatics of Pelé in his final World Cup. "We jumped together," said Burgnich, the Italian defender who marked

him, "but when I landed, I could see Pelé was still floating in
the air."

Four world champions, Brazil, Italy, Germany and
Uruguay, waged the semi-finals. Germany took third place,
Uruguay fourth. In the final, Brazil astonished Italy by winning 4-1. The British press commented: "Such beautiful soccer ought to be outlawed." People stand up to tell the story of
the final goal: the ball travelled through all Brazil, each of the
eleven players touched it, and at last Pelé, without even looking, laid it out on a silver platter for Carlos Alberto coming in
like a tornado to make the kill.

"Torpedo" Müller from Germany led the list of scorers
with ten, followed by the Brazilian Jairzinho with seven.

Undefeated champions for the third time, Brazil kept the
Rimet Cup for good. At the end of 1983 the cup was stolen
and sold after being melted down to nearly two kilos of pure
gold. In the display case, a copy stands in its place.

goal by jairzinho

IT WAS at the '70 World Cup. Brazil was playing England.

Tostão got the ball from Paulo César and scurried ahead as
far as he could, but all of England was spread out in the penalty area. Even the Queen was there. Tostão eluded one, then

another and one more, then he passed the ball to Pelé. Three players suffocated him on the spot. Pelé pretended to press on and the three opponents went for the smoke. He put on the brakes, pivoted and left the ball on the feet of Jairzinho, who was racing in. Jairzinho had learned to shake off his markers on the sandlots of the toughest slums of Rio de Janeiro: he came on like a black bullet and evaded one Englishman, before the ball, a white bullet, crossed the goal line defended by the . keeper Banks.

It was the winning goal. Swaying to the rhythm of a fiesta, Brazil's attackers had tossed off seven guardians of the steel fortress, which simply melted under the hot breeze blowing from the south.

the fiesta

THERE ARE TOWNS and villages in Brazil which have no church, but not a one lacks a soccer field. Sunday is the day of hard labor for cardiologists across the country. On a normal Sunday people die of excitement during the mass of the ball. On a Sunday without soccer, people die of boredom.

When the Brazilian national team met disaster in the '66 World Cup, there were suicides, nervous breakdowns, flags at half-mast and black ribbons on doors. A procession of dancing mourners filled the streets to bury the country's soccer prowess in a coffin. Four years later, Brazil won the world championship for the third time and Nelson Rodrigues wrote that Brazilians were no longer afraid of being carried off by the dog-catcher, they were all ermine-caped kings in pointy crowns.

In the '70 World Cup, Brazil played a soccer worthy of her people's yearning for celebration and craving for beauty. All the world was suffering from the mediocrity of defensive soccer which had the entire side hanging back to maintain the *catenaccio* while one or two men played by themselves up front. Risk and creative spontaneity weren't allowed. Brazil, however, was astonishing: a team on the attack, playing with four strikers, Jairzinho, Tostão, Pelé and Rivelino, sometimes increased to five and even six when Gerson and Carlos Alberto came up from the back. That steamroller pulverized Italy in the final.

A quarter of a century later, such audacity would be considered suicide. In the '94 World Cup, Brazil won another final against Italy, this time decided in a penalty shoot-out after 120 minutes without a single goal. If it hadn't been for the penalty goals, the nets would have remained untouched for all eternity.

soccer and the generals

AT THE VICTORY carnival in 1970, General Médici, dictator of Brazil, handed out cash to the players, posed for photographers with the trophy in his arms, and even headed a ball for the cameras. The march composed for the team, "Forward Brazil," became the government's anthem, while the image of Pelé soaring above the field was used in TV ads that proclaimed: "No one can stop Brazil." When Argentina won the World Cup in 1978, General Videla used the image of Kempes, unstoppable as a hurricane, for exactly the same purpose.

Soccer is the fatherland, soccer is power: "I am the fatherland," these military dictatorships were saying.

Meanwhile, Chile's bigwig General Pinochet named himself president of Colo-Colo, the most popular club in the country, and General García Meza, who had taken over Bolivia, named himself president of Wilstermann, a club with a multitude of fervent fans.

Soccer is the people, soccer is power: "I am the people," these military dictatorships were saying.

blinks

EDUARDO ANDRÉS Maglioni, forward for the Argentine club
Independiente, won a spot in the Guinness Book of World
Records as the player who scored the most goals in the least time.

In 1973, at the beginning of the second half of a match
against Gimnasia y Esgrima from La Plata, Maglioni beat
the goalkeeper Guruciaga three times in one minute and
fifty seconds.

goal by maradona

IT WAS 1973. The juvenile teams of Argentinos Juniors and
River Plate faced off in Buenos Aires.

Number 10 for Argentinos received the ball from his
keeper, evaded River's center forward and took off. Several
players tried to block his path: he put it over the first one's
tail, between the legs of the second, and he fooled the third
with a backheel. Then, without a pause, he paralyzed the
defenders, left the keeper sprawled on the ground, and walked
the ball into the net. On the field stood seven crushed boys
and four more with their mouths agape.

That kid's team, the Cebollitas, went undefeated for a
hundred games and caught the attention of the press. One of

the players, "Poison," who was thirteen, declared: "We play for fun. We'll never play for money. When there's money in it, everybody kills themselves to be a star and that's when jealousy and selfishness take over."

As he spoke he had his arm around the best-loved player of all, who was also the shortest and the happiest: Diego Armando Maradona, who was twelve and had just scored that incredible goal.

Maradona had the habit of sticking out his tongue when he was on the attack. All his goals were scored with his tongue out. By night he slept with his arms around a ball and by day he performed miracles with it. He lived in a poor home in a poor neighborhood and he wanted to be an industrial technician.

the 1974 world cup

PRESIDENT NIXON was on the ropes, weak-kneed, buffeted ceaselessly by the Watergate scandal, while a spaceship was hurtling toward Jupiter. In Washington, an army lieutenant who had murdered a hundred civilians in Vietnam was found innocent: after all there weren't more than a hundred, and they were civilians and, what's more, they were Vietnamese.

The novelists Miguel Angel Asturias and Pär Lakgervist lay dying, as did the painter David Alfaro Siqueiros. And

General Perón, who had burned his mark on Argentina's history, was on his deathbed. Dying, too, was Duke Ellington, the king of jazz. The daughter of the king of the press, Patricia Hearst, was falling in love with her kidnappers, robbing banks and denouncing her father as a bourgeois pig. Well-informed sources in Miami announced the imminent fall of Fidel Castro, it was only a matter of hours.

The Greek dictatorship was crumbling, and so was the one in Portugal, where the Revolution of the Carnations stepped out dancing to the beat of "Grandola, vila morena." The dictatorship of Augusto Pinochet was tightening its grip on Chile, while in Spain Francisco Franco was dying in the Francisco Franco Hospital, sick with power and age.

In a historic plebiscite, Italians were voting to legalize divorce, which seemed preferable to daggers, poison and other methods favored by tradition to resolve marital disputes. In a no less historic vote, the leaders of world soccer were electing João Havelange president of FIFA, and while in Switzerland Havelange was ousting the prestigious Stanley Rous, in Germany the tenth World Cup was getting underway.

A brand new cup was on display. Though uglier than the Rimet Cup, it was nonetheless coveted by nine teams from Europe and five from the Americas, plus Australia and Zaire. The Soviet Union had lost out in the run-up because they refused to play a qualifying game in Chile's National Stadium, which not long before had been a concentration camp and the site of executions by firing squad. So in that stadium the Chilean squad played the most pathetic match in the history of soccer: they played against no one, scored several goals on the empty net, and were cheered by the crowd. During the World Cup, Chile didn't win a single match.

Surprise: the Dutch players brought their wives or girl-friends with them to Germany and stayed with them throughout the tournament. It was the first time such a thing had happened. Another surprise: the Dutch had wings on their feet and reached the final undefeated, with fourteen goals in their favor and only one against, which out of sheer bad luck had been scored by one of their own. The '74 World Cup revolved around the "Clockwork Orange," the over-whelming creation of Cruyff, Neeskens, Rensenbrink, Krol and the other indefatigable Dutch players driven by coach Rinus Michels.

At the beginning of the final match, Cruyff exchanged colors with Beckenbauer. And then the third surprise occurred: "The Kaiser" and his team punctured the Dutch party balloon. Maier who blocked everything, Müller who scored everything, and Breitner who solved everything poured two buckets of cold water on the favorites, and against all odds the Germans won 2-1. The history of the '54 Cup in Switzerland, when Germany beat the unbeatable Hungary, was repeated.

Behind West Germany and Holland came Poland. In fourth place Brazil, who did not manage to be what they could have been. A Polish player, Lato, ended up as leading scorer with seven, followed by another Pole, Szarmach, and the Dutchman Neeskens with five apiece.

cruyff

THEY CALLED the Dutch team the "Clockwork Orange," but there was nothing mechanical about this work of imagination that left everyone befuddled with its incessant changes. Like River's "Machine," another team libeled by its nickname, this orange fire flitted back and forth, fanned by an all-knowing breeze that sped it forward and pulled it back. Everyone attacked and everyone defended, deploying and retreating in a vertiginous fan. Faced with a team in which each one was all eleven, the opposing players lost their step.

A Brazilian reporter called it "organized disorganization." Holland had music and the one who carried the melody, keeping so many simultaneous notes on pitch and in tune, was Johan Cruyff. Conducting the orchestra and playing his own instrument at the same time, Cruyff worked harder than anyone.

This scrawny live-wire earned a spot on the Ajax roster when he was only a child: while his mother waited on tables at the club bar, he collected balls that went off the field, shined the players' shoes and placed the flags in the corners. He did everything they asked of him and nothing they ordered him to do. He wanted to play and they wouldn't let him because his body was too weak and his will too strong. When they finally gave him a chance, he took it and never let it go. Still a boy, he made his debut on the Dutch team, played stupendously, scored a goal and knocked out the referee with one punch.

From that night on he kept up his reputation for being tempestuous, hardworking and talented. Over two decades he won twenty-two championships in Holland and Spain. He retired when he was thirty-seven after scoring his final goal, and the crowd carried him on its shoulders from the stadium to his house.

müller

THE COACH of club TSV in Munich told him: "You won't go far in soccer. Better try something else."

Back then, Gerd Müller worked twelve hours a day in a textile mill.

Eleven years later, in 1974, this stumpy tub of a player was champion of the world. No one scored more goals than he in the history of either the German league or the national team.

Nobody saw a wild wolf on the field. Disguised as an old woman, his fangs and claws hidden, he strolled along, making a show of showering innocent passes and other works of charity. Meanwhile, he slipped unnoticed into the box. The net was the bridal veil of an irresistible girl. In front of the open goal he licked his chops. And in one fell swoop he stood naked, then bit.

havelange

IN 1974, after a long climb, Jean Marie Faustin de Godefroid Havelange reached the summit of FIFA. And he announced: "I have come to sell a product named soccer."

From that point on, Havelange has exercised absolute power over the world of soccer. With his body glued to the throne, he reigns in his palace in Zurich surrounded by a court of voracious technocrats. He governs more countries than the United Nations, travels more than the Pope, and has more medals than any war hero.

Havelange was born in Brazil, where he is the owner of Cometa, the country's largest transport company, and other businesses specializing in financial speculation, weapons sales and life insurance. But his opinions don't seem very Brazilian. A journalist from *The Times* in London once asked him: "What do you like best about soccer? The glory? The beauty? The poetry? Winning?"

And he answered: "The discipline."

This old-style monarch has transformed the geography of soccer and made it into one of the more splendid multinational businesses in the world. Under his rule, the number of countries competing in world championships has doubled: there were sixteen in 1974; there will be thirty-two in 1998. And from what we can decipher through the fog around his balance sheets, the profits generated by these tournaments have multiplied so prodigiously that the Biblical miracle of bread and fish seems like a joke in comparison.

The new protagonists of world soccer, countries in Africa,

the Middle East and Asia, offer Havelange a broad base of support, but his power gains sustenance, above all, from his association with several gigantic corporations, Coca-Cola and Adidas among them. It was Havelange who convinced Adidas to finance the candidacy of his friend Juan Antonio Samaranch for the presidency of the International Olympic Committee in 1980. Samaranch, who during the Franco dictatorship had the good sense to wear a blue shirt and salute with his palm extended, is now the other king of world sport. These two manage enormous sums of money. How much, no one knows. They are rather bashful about the subject.

the owners of the ball

FIFA, which holds court in Zurich, the International Olympic Committee, which rules from Lausanne, and ISL Marketing, which runs things from Lucerne, manage the World Cup and the Olympics. All three of these powerful organizations maintain their head offices in Switzerland, a country famous for William Tell's marksmanship, precision watches and religious devotion to bank secrecy. Coincidentally, all three profess an extraordinary degree of modesty when it comes to the money which passes through their hands, and that which in their hands remains.

ISL Marketing owns exclusive rights on stadium advertising, films and videos, logos, banners and mascots for international soccer competitions until the end of the century. This business belongs to the inheritors of Adolph Dassler, founder of Adidas, brother and enemy of the founder of its competitor Puma. When Havelange and Samaranch offered a sales monopoly to the Dassler family, they were acting out of gratitude, a noble sentiment. Adidas, the largest sports-clothing manufacturer in the world, had shown considerable generosity when it came to helping Havelange and Samaranch consolidate their personal power. In 1990, the Dasslers sold Adidas to French businessman Bernard Tapie, but held on to ISL, which the family still controls today in association with the Japanese advertising firm Dentsu.

Control over world sport is no small potatoes. At the end of 1994, speaking in New York to a businessmen's group, Havelange confessed a few numbers, something he rarely does: "I can confirm that soccer generates a total of $225 billion world wide every year." He boasted that such a fortune compared favorably to the $136 billion in sales that General Motors, the world's largest multinational corporation, recorded in 1993.

In the same speech, Havelange warned: "Soccer is a commercial product that must be sold as wisely as possible." And he cited the first law of wisdom in today's world: "You have to pay a lot of attention to the packaging."

The sale of television rights is the most productive vein in the fantastically rich mine of international competitions, and FIFA and the International Olympic Committee enjoy the lion's share of the proceeds. That money has multiplied spectacularly since television began to broadcast world championships live around the world. The 1993 Barcelona Olympics earned six-hundred-and-thirty times as much from television as the Rome Olympics in 1960, when the broadcast did not reach beyond the national market.

When it comes to deciding which companies will be the advertisers for each competition, Havelange, Samaranch and the Dassler family never quarrel. The machine that turns all passion into money can't afford the luxury of promoting the most healthy or useful products for active sports fans. They simply place themselves at the service of the highest bidder, and they only want to know if Mastercard will pay more than Visa, and if Fujifilm will put more money on the table than Kodak. Coca-Cola, that nutritious elixir no athlete's body can do without, always heads the list. Its wealth of virtues place it beyond question.

With *fin-de-siècle* soccer so wrapped up in marketing and sponsors, it's no surprise that some of Europe's biggest clubs are actually companies that belong to other companies. Juventus from Turin, just like Fiat, is part of the Agnelli Group. Milan belongs to the constellation of three hundred companies of the Berlusconi Group. Parma belongs to Parmalat. Sampdoria, to the oil conglomerate Mantovani. Fiorentina, to the movie production company Cecchi Gori. Olympique of Marseilles moved to the forefront of European soccer when it became one of Bernard Tapie's companies, until a bribery scandal ruined his successful career. Paris Saint-Germain belongs to the television firm Canal Plus.

Sochaux's sponsor, Peugeot, also owns the club stadium. Philips owns the Dutch club PSV in Eindhoven. Bayer is the name of the two German first division clubs the company finances: Bayer Leverkusen and Bayer Uerdingen. The inventor and owner of Anstrad computers is also the proprietor of the British club Tottenham Hotspur, whose shares are traded on the stock exchange; Blackburn Rovers belongs to the Walker Group.

In Japan, where professional soccer is still young, the largest companies have set up their own teams and hired foreign stars, making the safe bet that soccer is a universal language for advertising their businesses the world over. Furukawa electric company started the club Jef United Ichihara and hired German superstar Pierre Littbarski and the Czechs Frantisek and Pavel. Toyota set up club Grampus, who signed on English striker Gary Lineker. The veteran but ever-brilliant Zico played for Kashima, which belongs to the Sumitomo industrial-financial conglomerate. Mazda, Mitsubishi, Nissan, Panasonic and Japan Airlines also have soccer teams.

These teams can lose money, but that doesn't matter as long as they project a good image for the corporate proprietors. That's why their ownership is no secret: soccer helps advertise the companies and in all the world there is no greater public-relations tool. When Silvio Berlusconi bought Milan, which was in bankruptcy, he launched the new chapter in its life with all the choreography of a major advertising campaign. That afternoon in 1987, Milan's eleven players descended slowly from a helicopter hovering above the center of the field, while loudspeakers blared Wagner's "Walkyrie." Bernard Tapie, another specialist in his own protagonism, liked to celebrate Olympique's victories with huge parties, glowing with fireworks and laser beams, where top rock groups performed.

Soccer, the fountain of so much passion, also generates fame and power. The teams that enjoy some autonomy because they don't depend directly on other companies are often run by shady businessmen or second-rate politicians who use the game as a prestigious platform to catapult themselves into the public eye. There are also rare cases where just the opposite is true: men who put their well-earned fame at the service of soccer, like the English singer Elton John, who bought Watford, the team he loved, or the movie director Francisco Lombardi, who runs Peru's Sporting Cristal.

jesus

IN THE MIDDLE of 1969, a large hall for weddings, baptisms and conventions opened in Spain's Guadarrama mountains. While the grand opening banquet was in full swing, the floor collapsed, the roof fell in and the guests were buried in rubble. Fifty-two people died. The hall had been built with public funds, but without permits, licenses or an architect in charge.

The owner and builder of the ephemeral edifice, Jesus Gil y Gil, went to jail. He spent two years and three months behind bars—two weeks for each death—until he was pardoned by Generalissimo Franco. As soon as he set foot out of prison, Jesus was back to serve the progress of the fatherland once again in the construction industry.

Some time later, this businessman became the owner of a soccer team, Atlético of Madrid. Thanks to soccer, which turned him into a popular television personality, Jesus was able to launch a political career. In 1991 he was elected mayor of Marbella, winning more votes than anyone else in the country. During his election campaign he promised to clear thieves, drunks and drug addicts off the streets of this tourist spot reserved for the amusement of Arab sheiks and foreign gangsters specializing in gun-running and drug trafficking.

Atlético of Madrid remains the base of his power and prestige, even though the team frequently loses. Coaches don't last more than a few weeks. Jesus Gil y Gil seeks advice from his horse Imperioso, a snow-white and very sentimental stallion.

"Imperioso, we lost."

"I know, Gil."

"Whose fault is it?"

"I don't know, Gil."

"Yes you do, Imperioso. It's the coach's fault."

"So, fire him."

the 1978 world cup

IN GERMANY, the popular Volkswagen Beetle was dying; in England, the first test tube baby was being born; in Italy, abortion was being made legal. The first victims of AIDS, a disease not yet called that, were succumbing. The Red Brigades were killing Aldo Moro; the United States was promising to give Panama back the canal it stole at the beginning of the century. Well-informed sources in Miami announced the imminent fall of Fidel Castro, it was only a matter of hours. In Nicaragua the Somoza dynasty was teetering, in Iran the Shah's dynasty was teetering, the Guatemalan military were machine-gunning a crowd of peasants in the town of Panzós. Domitila Barrios and four other women from tin-mining communities were launching a hunger strike against Bolivia's military dictatorship, and soon all Bolivia was on a hunger strike: the dictatorship was falling. The Argentine military dictatorship, in contrast, remained in good health, and to prove it played host to the eleventh World Cup.

Ten European countries, four from the Americas, plus Iran and Tunisia, took part. The Pope sent his blessings from Rome. To the strains of a military march, General Videla pinned a medal on Havelange during the opening ceremonies in Buenos Aires's Monumental Stadium. A few steps away, Argentina's Auschwitz, the torture and extermination camp at the Navy School of Mechanics, was operating at full speed. A few miles beyond that, prisoners were being thrown alive from airplanes into the sea.

"At last the world can see the true face of Argentina," crowed the president of FIFA to the TV cameras. Special guest Henry Kissinger predicted: "This country has a great future in all ways." And the captain of the German team, Berti Vogts, who made the first kick-off, declared a few days later: "Argentina is a country where order reigns. I haven't seen any political prisoners."

The home team won a few games, but lost to Italy and drew with Brazil. To reach the final against Holland, they had to drown Peru in a flood of goals. Argentina got more than they needed, but the massacre, 6-0, sowed doubt among skeptical fans and magnanimous ones, too. The Peruvians were stoned on their return to Lima.

The final between Argentina and Holland was decided in extra time. The Argentines won 3-1 and in a way their victory came thanks to the patriotism of the post that saved the Argentine net in the last minute of regular play. That post, which stopped a resounding blast by Rensenbrink, was never given military honors only because of the nature of human ingratitude. In any case, more important than the post, as it turned out, were the goals of Mario Kempes, an unstoppable colt who liked to gallop over the grass covered with a snow-fall of confetti, his hair flying in the wind.

When they handed out the trophies, the Dutch players refused to salute the leaders of the Argentine dictatorship. Third place went to Brazil, fourth to Italy.

Kempes was voted best player in the Cup and was also the leading scorer with six goals. Behind him came the Peruvian Cubillas and Rensenbrink of Holland with five apiece.

happiness

FIVE THOUSAND journalists from all over the world, a sumptuous media center, impeccable stadiums, new airports: a model of efficiency. Veteran German reporters confessed that the '78 World Cup reminded them of the '36 Olympics in Berlin for which Hitler had pulled out all the stops.

The cost was a state secret. Many millions of dollars were spent and lost—how many, it was never known—so that the smiles of a happy country under military tutelage would be broadcast to the four corners of the earth. Meanwhile, the top brass who organized the World Cup carried on with their plan of extermination, for reasons of war or just to be sure. "The final solution," as they called it, murdered thousands of Argentinians without leaving a trace—how many, it was never known: anyone who tried to find out was swallowed up by the earth. Curiosity was, like dissent, like any question, absolute proof of subversion. The president of the Argentine Rural Society, Celedonio Pereda, declared that thanks to soccer, "There will be no more of the defamation that certain well-known Argentinians have spread through the Western media with the profits from their robberies and kidnappings." You couldn't even criticize the players, not even the coach. The Argentine team stumbled a few times in the championship, but local commentators were obliged to do nothing but applaud.

To make over its international image, the dictatorship paid an American public relations firm half-a-million dollars. The report from the experts at Burson-Masteller was titled:

"What is True for Products, is Also True for Countries."
Admiral Carlos Alberto Lacoste, the strongman of the World
Cup, explained in an interview: "If I go to Europe or to the
United States, what will impress me most? Large buildings,
big airports, terrific cars, fancy candies ..."

The Admiral, an illusionist skilled at making dollars
evaporate and sudden fortunes appear, took the reins of the
World Cup after the previous officer in charge was mysteri-
ously assassinated. Lacoste managed immense sums of
money without any oversight and it seems, because he wasn't
paying close attention, he ended up keeping some of the
change. Even the dictatorship's Treasury Secretary, Juan
Alemann, took note of the squandering of public funds and
asked a few inconvenient questions. The Admiral had the
habit of warning: "Later on, don't complain if somebody
plants a bomb ..."

A bomb did explode in Alemann's house at the very
moment when Argentinians were celebrating their fourth
goal against Peru.

When the Cup was over, out of gratitude for his hard
work, Admiral Lacoste was named vice-president of FIFA.

goal by gemmill

IT WAS at the '78 World Cup. Holland, who was doing well, played against Scotland, who was doing poorly.

Scottish player Archibald Gemmill got the ball from his countryman Hartford and was polite enough to ask the Dutch to dance to the tune of a lone bagpiper.

Wildschut was the first to fall, his head spinning, at Gemmill's feet. Then he left Suurbier reeling in the dust. Krol had it worse: Gemmill put it between his legs. And when the keeper Jongbloed came at him, the Scot lobbed the ball over his head.

goal by bettega

IT WAS at the '78 World Cup. Italy defeated the home team 1-0.

The play that set up Italy's goal drew a perfect triangle on the field, inside which the Argentine defenders were left as lost as blind men in a shoot-out. Antognoni slid the ball over to Bettega, who slapped it toward Rossi, who had his back to him. Rossi returned it with a backheel while Bettega infiltrated the box. Bettega then overpowered two players and beat the keeper Fillol with a tremendous left.

Though no one knew it then, the Italian team had

already begun to win the World Cup that would take place four years later.

goal by sunderland

IT WAS 1979. At Wembley Stadium, Arsenal and Manchester United were battling the final of the English FA Cup.

A good match, but nothing aroused suspicions that this would suddenly turn into the most electric final of all that had occurred in the Cup's long history since 1871. Arsenal was ahead 2-0 and the game was nearly over. The game was decided and people began to leave the stadium. Suddenly a cloudburst of goals was let loose. *Three goals in two minutes*: a sure shot by McQueen was followed by a pretty penetration by McIlroy, who eluded two defenders and the keeper, giving United the equalizers between the 86th and 87th minutes. But before the 88th minute was over Arsenal regained the lead. Liam Brady, who as usual was the outstanding player of the game, put together the final play, and Alan Sunderland took a clean shot to make it 3-2.

the 1982 world cup

"MEFISTO" BY István Szabó, a masterpiece of art and betrayal, was winning an Oscar in Hollywood, while in Germany the life of the tormented and talented movie director Fassbinder was snuffed out early. Romy Schneider was committing suicide, Sophia Loren was being imprisoned for tax evasion. In Poland trade unionist Lech Walesa was on his way to jail.

García Márquez was accepting the Nobel in the name of the poets, beggars, musicians, prophets, warriors and rascals of Latin America. An army massacre of a village in El Salvador: in a hail of bullets more then seven hundred peasants died, half of them children. In Guatemala, General Ríos Montt was taking power to multiply the butchery of Indians—he proclaimed that God had given him the country's reins and announced that the Holy Spirit would direct his secret service.

Egypt was recovering the Sinai Peninsula, ocuppied by Israel since the Six Day War. The first artificial heart was beating in someone's breast. Well-informed sources in Miami announced the imminent fall of Fidel Castro, it was a matter of hours. In Italy, the Pope survived a second assassination attempt. In Spain, the officers who had organized the attack on Congress were getting thirty years and Felipe González was launching his impressive race for the presidency, when in Barcelona the twelfth World Cup got underway.

Twenty-four countries took part, eight more than in the previous Cup, but the Americas did not gain a larger quota: there were fourteen teams from Europe, six from the Americas and two from Africa, plus Kuwait and New Zealand.

On the first day, world champions Argentina lost in Barcelona. A few hours later, far from there in the Falkland Islands, the Argentine brass were defeated in their war against England. These brave generals, who over several years of dictatorship had won the war against their own countrymen, surrendered like lambs to the British. The image was broadcast on television: navy officer Alfredo Astiz, violator of every human right, hung his head and signed the humiliating surrender on the island of South Georgia.

During the days that followed, the TV showed images of the '82 Cup: the billowing tunic of Sheik Fahid Al-Ahmad Al-Sabah, who ran onto the field to protest a goal by France against Kuwait; the goal by Englishman Bryan Robson after half a minute, the quickest in the Cup history; the indifference of German keeper Schumacher after he knocked out the French striker Battiston with his knee. (Before becoming a goalkeeper, Schumacher had been a blacksmith.)

Europe won the top spots in the tournament, although Brazil played the best soccer on the feet of Zico, Falcão and Sócrates. The Brazilian team was out of luck, but they delighted the crowd and Zico, who had just won the title of best player in South America, justified once again the "Zicomania" in the stands.

The Cup went to Italy. The Italian team started off badly, stumbling from tie to tie, but it finally took flight, thanks to its overall cohesion and the opportune machine-gun blasts of Paolo Rossi. In the final against Germany, Italy won 3-1.

Poland, guided by Boniek's fine music, took third place. Fourth went to France, who deserved better for the

European effectiveness and African joy of its memorable midfield.

The Italian Rossi led the list of scorers with six goals, followed by the German Rummenigge, who scored five and set the team on fire.

pears from an elm

ALAIN GIRESSE, along with Platini, Tigana and Genghini, made up the most spectacular midfield of the '82 World Cup and in the entire history of French soccer. Giresse was so small that on the TV screen he always appeared to be in the distance.

The Hungarian Puskas was short and fat like the German Seeler. The Dutchman Cruyff and the Italian Gianni Rivera were skinny. Pelé had flat feet, as did Néstor Rossi, Argentina's solid center-half. The Brazilian Rivelino had the worst score on the Cooper test, but on the field no one could catch him. His countryman Sócrates had the body of a heron, long bony legs and small feet that tired easily, but he was such a master of the backheel he even used it for penalty kicks.

Whoever believes physical size and tests of speed or strength have anything to do with soccer prowess are sorely mistaken. Just as mistaken as those who believe that IQ tests have anything to do with talent or that there is a relationship between penis size and sexual pleasure. Good soccer players need not be titans sculpted by Michaelangelo. In soccer, skill is much more important than shape, and in many cases skill is the art of turning limitations into virtues.

The Colombian Carlos Valderrama has warped feet, and the curvature helps him hide the ball. It's the same story with Garrincha's twisted feet. Where is the ball? In his ear? Inside his shoe? Where did it go? The Uruguayan "Cocacho" Alvarez, who walked with a limp, had one foot pointing toward the other, and he was one of the few defenders who could stop Pelé without punching or kicking him.

Two short chubby players, Romario and Maradona, were the stars of the '94 World Cup. And two Uruguayan strikers who in recent years have become stars in Italy, Ruben Sosa and Carlos Aguilera, have a similar physique. Thanks to their diminutive size, the Brazilian Leônidas, the Englishman Kevin Keegan, the Irishman George Best and the Dutchman Allan Simonsen, known as "The Flea," all managed to slip through impenetrable defenses and scurry easily by huge fullbacks who hit them with all they had but couldn't stop them. Also tiny but well-armored was Félix Loustau, left wing for River Plate's "Machine." They called him "The Ventilator" because he was the one who allowed the rest of the squad to catch their breath by making the opposing players chase him. Lilliputians can change speed and accelerate brusquely without falling, because they aren't built like skyscrapers.

platini

MICHEL PLATINI did not have an athlete's physique. In 1972 the Metz club doctor told Platini he was suffering from "a weak heart and poor respiratory capacity." The report was enough for Metz to reject this aspiring player, even though the doctor didn't notice that Platini's ankles were stiff and easily fractured and that he tended to put on weight due to his passion for pasta. In any case, ten years later, shortly before the World Cup in Spain, this defective reject got his revenge: his team, Saint Etienne, beat Metz 9-2.

Platini was the synthesis of the best of French soccer: he had the aim of Justo Fontaine, who in the '58 World Cup scored thirteen goals, a record never beaten, along with the mobility and astuteness of Raymond Kopa. In each match Platini not only put on a magic show of goals, ones that couldn't possibly be real, but he also set crowds on fire with his ability to organize the plays of the entire side. Under his leadership, the French team played a harmonious soccer, fashioned and relished step by step as each play grew: precisely the opposite of center to the box, all-out stampede and God have mercy.

In the semi-finals of the '82 World Cup, France lost to Germany on a penalty shoot-out. That match was a duel between Platini and Rummenigge, who was injured but leapt onto the field anyway and won the game. Later on, in the final, Germany lost to Italy. Neither Platini nor Rummenigge, two players who made soccer history, ever had the pleasure of winning a world championship.

pagan sacrifices

IN 1985, fanatics of unfortunate renown killed thirty-nine Italian fans on the terraces of the old Heysel stadium in Brussels. The English club Liverpool was playing Juventus from Italy in the European Cup final when the hooligans went on the rampage. The Italian fans, cornered against a wall, were trampled among themselves or thrown into an abyss. Television broadcast the butchery live with the game, which was not suspended.

After that, Italy was off-limits to English fans, even those that carried proof of a good up-bringing. In the 1990 World Cup, Italy had no choice but to allow fans onto Cerdeña Island where the English team was to play, but there were more Scotland Yard agents among them than soccer addicts, and the British minister of sport personally took charge of keeping an eye on them.

One century earlier, in 1890, *The Times* in London warned: "Our 'Hooligans' go from bad to worse . . . the worse circumstance is that they multiply . . . the 'Hooligan is a hideous excrescence on our civilization." Today, such excrescence continues to perpetrate crimes under the pretext of soccer.

Wherever hooligans appear, they sow panic. Their bodies are plastered with tatoos on the outside and alcohol on the inside. Patriotic odds and ends hang from their necks and ears, they use brass knuckles and truncheons, and sweat oceans of violence while howling "Rule Britannia" and other rancors from the lost Empire. In England and in other countries, these killers also frequently brandish Nazi symbols and proclaim their hatred of blacks, Arabs, Turks, Pakistanis or Jews.

"Go back to Africa," roared one Real Madrid "ultra" who enjoyed shouting insults at blacks "because they've come to take away my job."

Under the pretext of soccer, Italian "naziskins" whistle at black players and call the enemy fans "Jews." "Ebrei!" they shout.

Rowdy crowds that insult soccer the way drunks insult wine are not exclusive to Europe. Nearly every country suffers from them, some more, some less, and over time the rabid dogs have multiplied. Until a few years ago, Chile had the friendliest fans I've ever seen: men and women and children who sang in the stands, with musical competitions that even had judges. Today the Chilean club Colo-Colo has its own gang of troublemakers, "The White Claw," and the gang from the University of Chile team is called "The Underdogs."

In 1993 Jorge Valdano calculated that during the previous fifteen years over a hundred people had been killed by violence in Argentina's stadiums. Violence, Valdano said, grows in direct proportion to social injustice and the frustrations people face in their daily lives. Everywhere, gangs attract young people tormented by the lack of jobs and the lack of hope. A few months after he said this, the Buenos Aires club Boca Juniors was defeated 2-0 by River Plate, their traditional rival. Leaving the stadium, two River fans were shot dead. "We tied 2-2," commented a young Boca fan interviewed on TV.

In a column he wrote in other times about other sports, Dione Crisóstomo painted a portrait of Roman fans of the second century after Christ: "When they go to the stadium, it's as if they had discovered a cache of drugs. They forget about themselves entirely and without a drop of shame they say and do the first thing that comes into their heads." The worst catastrophe in the history of sport occured there, in Rome, four centuries later. In the year 512, thousands died—they say thirty thousand, though it's hard to believe—in a street war between two groups of fans that lasted several days. They weren't fans of soccer, but of chariot racing.

In soccer stadiums, the tragedy with the most victims occurred in 1964 in the capital of Peru. When the referee disallowed a goal in the final minutes of a match against Argentina, oranges, beer cans and other projectiles rained down from the stands burning with rage. The police responded with tear gas and bullets which provoked a stampede. A police charge crushed the crowd against the exit gates, which were closed. More than three hundred died. That night a multitude protested in the streets of Lima: the demonstration was against the referee, not the police.

the 1986 world cup

BABY DOC Duvalier fled Haiti, taking everything with him. Also stealing and fleeing was Ferdinand Marcos of the Philippines, while U.S. sources revealed, better late than never, that this much-praised Philippine hero of the Second World War had actually been a deserter.

Haley's Comet was visiting our skies after a long absence, nine moons were being discovered around the planet Uranus, and the first hole was appearing in the ozone layer that protects us from the sun. A new antileukemia drug, a daughter of genetic engineering, came on the market. In Japan a popular singer committed suicide, and following her lead twenty-three of her fans chose death. An earthquake left two hundred thousand Salvadorans homeless and a catastrophe in the Soviet nuclear plant at Chernobyl unleashed a cloudburst of radioactive poison, impossible to measure or to stop, over who knows how many miles and people.

Felipe González said *Sí* to NATO, the Atlantic military alliance, after having screamed *No*, and a plebiscite blessed the about-face while Spain and Portugal entered the European Common Market. The world was mourning the death of Olof Palme, Sweden's prime minister, who was assassinated in the street. A time of mourning for the arts and letters: among those who left us were the sculptor Henry Moore and the writers Simone de Beauvoir, Jean Genet, Juan Rulfo and Jorge Luis Borges.

The Irangate scandal was exploding, implicating President Reagan, the CIA and Nicaraguan *contras* in gun-running and drug-trafficking; also exploding was the spaceship Challenger on takeoff from Cape Canaveral with seven crew-members on board. The U.S. Air Force was bombing Libya, killing a daughter of Colonel Gaddafi, to punish him for an attack that years later was found to have been perpetrated by Iran.

In a Lima jail, four hundred prisoners were being lined up and shot. Well-informed sources in Miami announced the imminent fall of Fidel Castro, it was a matter of hours. Many buildings without proper foundations but with lots of people inside fell when an earthquake struck Mexico City the previous year and a good part of the city was still in ruins, when the thirteenth World Cup got underway there.

Participating were fourteen European countries and six from the Americas, as well as Morocco, South Korea, Iraq and Algeria. The "wave" was born in the stands at the Mexico Cup, and ever since it has moved fans the world over to the rhythm of a rough sea. There were matches that made your hair stand on end, like France against Brazil where the unfailing Platini, Zico and Sócrates failed on penalty kicks. And there were two spectacular goal-fests involving Denmark: they scored six goals against Uruguay and suffered five against Spain.

But this was Maradona's World Cup. With two "lefty" goals against England, Maradona took revenge for the wound to his country's pride inflicted in the Falklands War: the first he converted with his left hand, which he called "the hand of God," and the other with his left foot, after having knocked the English defenders to the ground.

Argentina faced Germany in the final. It was Maradona who made the decisive pass that left Burruchaga alone with the ball when the clock was running out, so that Argentina could win 3-2 and take the championship. But before that another memorable goal had been scored: Valdano set off with the ball from the Argentine goal line, crossed the entire field and when Schumacher came out to meet him, he bounced the ball off the right post and into the net. Valdano talked to the ball as he came upfield, begging her: "Please, go in."

France took third place, followed by Belgium. Lineker of England led the list of scorers with six. Maradona scored five goals, as did Careca of Brazil and Butragueño of Spain.

the telecracy

TODAY THE stadium is a gigantic TV studio. The game is played for television so you can watch it at home. And television rules.

At the '86 World Cup, Valdano, Maradona and other players protested because the big matches were played at noon under a sun that fried everything it touched. Noon in Mexico, nightfall in Europe, that was the best time for European television. The German goalkeeper, Harald Schumacher, told the story: "I sweat. My throat is dry. The grass is like dried shit: hard, strange, hostile. The sun shines straight down on the stadium and strikes us right on the head. We cast no shadows. They say this is good for television."

Was the sale of the spectacle more important than the quality of play? The players are there to kick not to cry, and Havelange put an end to that maddening business: "They should play and shut their traps," he decreed.

Who ran the '86 World Cup? The Mexican Soccer Federation? No, please, no more intermediaries: it was run by Guillermo Cañedo, vice-president of Televisa and president of the company's international network. This World Cup belonged to Televisa, the private monopoly that owns the free time of all Mexicans and also owns Mexican soccer. And nothing could be more important than the money Televisa, along with FIFA, could earn from European broadcast rights. When a Mexican journalist had the insolent audacity to ask about the costs and profits of the World Cup, Cañedo cut him off cold: "This is a private company and we don't have to report to anybody."

When the World Cup ended, Cañedo continued as a Havelange courtesan occupying one of the vice-presidencies of FIFA, another private company that does not have to report to anybody.

Televisa not only holds the reins on national and international broadcasts of Mexican soccer, it also owns three first division clubs: América, the most powerful, Necaxa and Atlante.

In 1990 Televisa demonstrated the ferocious power it holds over the Mexican game. That year, the president of club Puebla, Emilio Maurer, had a deadly idea: it occurred to him that Televisa could easily put out more money for the exclusive rights to broadcast the games. Maurer's initiative was well-received by several leaders of the Mexican Soccer Federation. After all, the monopoly paid each club a little more than a thousand dollars, while amassing a fortune from advertising.

Televisa then showed them who was boss. Maurer was bombarded without mercy: overnight, creditors foreclosed on his companies and his home, he was threatened, assaulted, declared a fugitive from justice and a warrant was issued for his arrest. What's more, one nasty morning his club's stadium was closed down without warning. But gangster tactics weren't enough to make him come down off his high horse, so they had to put Maurer in jail and sweep him out of his rebel club and out of the Mexican Soccer Federation, along with all of his allies.

Throughout the world, by direct and indirect means, television decides where, when and how soccer will be played. The game has sold out to the small screen in body and soul and clothing too. Players are now TV stars. Who can compete with their shows? The program that had the largest audience in France and Italy in 1993 was the final of the European Cup-Winners' Cup between Olympique de Marseille and AC Milan. Milan, as we all know, belongs to Silvio Berlusconi, the czar of Italian television. Bernard Tapie was not the owner of French TV, but his club, Olympique, received from the small screen that year three hundred times more money than in 1980. He didn't lack any motive for affection.

Now milllions of people can watch matches, not only the thousands who fit into the stadiums. The number of fans has multiplied, as has the number of potential consumers of as many things as the image manipulators wish to sell. But unlike baseball and basketball, soccer is a game of continuous play that offers few interruptions for showing ads. The one half-time isn't sufficient. American television has proposed to correct this unpleasant defect by dividing the matches into four twenty-five minute periods—and Havelange agrees.

serious and in series

DON HOWE, coach of the English team, said in 1987: "A player who feels satisfied after losing a match could never be any good at soccer."

Professional soccer, ever more rapid, ever less beautiful, has tended to become a game of speed and strength, fueled by the fear of losing.

Players run a lot, and risk little or nothing. Audacity is not profitable. In forty years, between the '54 and the '94 World Cups, the average number of goals has fallen by half, even though in '94 an extra point was given for each victory to try to discourage ties. The highly praised efficiency of mediocrity: in modern soccer there are ever more teams made up of functionaries specialized in avoiding defeat, rather than players who run the risk of acting on inspiration and who allow their creative spirit to take charge.

The Chilean player Carlos Caszely made fun of greedy soccer: "It's the tactic of the bat," he said. "All eleven players hang from the crossbar."

And the Russian player Nikolai Starostin complained about remote-control soccer: "Now all the players look alike. If they changed shirts, no one would notice. They all play alike."

Playing seriously and playing in series, is that really playing? According to those who understand the root meaning of words, *to play* is to joke and *health* is when the body is as free as can be. The controlled effectiveness of mechanical repetitions, enemy of health, is making soccer sick.

To win without magic, without surprise or beauty, isn't that worse than losing? In 1994, during the Spanish championship, Real Madrid was defeated by Sporting from Gijón. But the men of Real Madrid played with *enthusiasm*, a word that originally meant "having the gods within." The coach, Jorge Valdano, beamed at the players in the dressing room: "When you play like that," he told them, "it's okay to lose."

running drug stores

IN THE '54 World Cup, when Germany burst out with such astonishing speed the Hungarians were left in the gutter, Ferenc Puskas said the German dressing room smelled like a garden of poppies. He claimed that had something to do with the fact that the winners ran like trains.

In 1987 Harald "Toni" Schumacher, the goalkeeper for the German national team, published a book in which he said: "There are too many drugs and not enough women," referring to German soccer and, by extension, to all professional teams. In *Der Anpfiff* ("The Starting Whistle"), Schumacher recounts that at the '86 World Cup the German players were given innumerable injections and pills and large doses of a mysterious mineral water that gave them diarrhea. Did that team represent its country or the German chemical industry? The players were even forced to take sleeping pills. Schumacher spat them out; to help him sleep he preferred beer.

The keeper confirmed that the consumption of anabolic steriods and stimulants is common in the professional game. Pressed by the law of productivity to win by any means necessary, many anxious and anguished players become running drug stores. And the same system that condemns them to that, also condemns them for that every time they get caught.

Schumacher, who admitted that he took drugs on occasion, was accused of treason. This popular idol, runner-up in two world championships, was knocked from his pedestal and dragged through the mud. Booted off his team, Cologne, he also lost his spot on the national squad and had no choice but to go and play in Turkey.

chants of scorn

IT'S NOT on any map but it's there. It's invisible, but there it is. A barrier that makes the memory of the Berlin Wall seem ridiculous: raised to separate those who have from those who need, it divides the globe into north and south, and draws borders within each country and each city. When the south of

174

the world commits the affront of scaling the walls and venturing where it shouldn't, the north reminds it, with truncheons, of its proper place. And the same thing happens to those who attempt to leave the zones of the damned in each country and each city.

Soccer, mirror of everything, reflects this reality. In the middle of the eighties, when Naples started playing the best soccer in Italy thanks to the magical influx of Maradona, fans in the north of the country reacted by unsheathing the old weapons of scorn. Neopolitans, usurpers of prohibited glory, were snatching trophies from the ever-powerful, and it was time to punish the insolence of the intruding scum of the south. In the stands of stadiums in Milan or Turin, banners insulted: "Neopolitans, welcome to Italy." Or they evoked cruelty: "Vesubio, we're counting on you."

And chants that were the children of fear and the grandchildren of racism resounded louder than ever:

What a stench, the dogs are running,
all because the Neopolitans are coming.
Oh cholerics buried by quake,
you've never seen soap, not even a cake,
Naples shit, Naples cholera,
you're the shame of all Italia.

In Argentina the same thing happens to Boca Juniors. Boca is the favorite of the spiky-haired dark-skinned poor who have invaded the lordly city of Buenos Aires in waves from the scrubby hinterlands and from neighboring countries. The enemy fans exorcize this fearful demon:

Boca's in mourning, everybody knows,
cause they're all black, they're all homos.
Kill the shit-kickers,
they aren't straight,
throw the bumpkins in the River Plate.

anything goes

IN 1988 Mexican journalist Miguel Angel Ramírez discovered a fountain of youth. Several players on Mexico's junior team who were two, three, even six years beyond the age limit, had been bathed in the magic waters: the directors falsified their birth certificates and fabricated false passports. The treatment was so effective that one player managed to become two years younger than his twin brother.

Then the vice-president of Guadalajara declared: "I won't say it's a good thing, but it's always been done."

And Rafael del Castillo, who was the top boss of junior soccer, asked: "Why can't Mexico be sneaky when other countries do it as a matter of course?"

Shortly after the '66 World Cup the comptroller of the Argentine Soccer Association, Valentín Suárez, declared: "Stanley Rous is a shady fellow. He ran the World Cup so that England would win. I'd do the same if the Cup were played in Argentina."

The morals of the market, which in our days are the morals of the world, give a green light to all keys to success, even if they're burglars' tools. Professional soccer has no scruples because it is part of an unscrupulous system of power that buys effectiveness at any price. And after all, scruples were never worth much. A "scruple" was the smallest measure of weight, the least significant, in Renaissance Italy. Five centuries later, Paul Steiner, a player for the German club Cologne, explained: "I play for money and for points. The opposing player wants to take my money and my points. That's why I ought to fight him by all means at my disposal."

And the Dutch player Ronald Koeman justified the brutal kick his compatriot Gillhaus gave the Frenchman Tigana in the stomach in 1988: "It was a class act. Tigana was their most dangerous player and he had to be neutralized at any cost."

The end justifies the means, and any beastly act is fine, though it's wise to do it on the sly. Basile Boli of Olympique de Marseille, a defender accused of mistreating others' ankles, spoke of his baptism by fire. In 1983 Roger Milla was elbowing him like crazy, so he flattened him with his head. "That was the first lesson: strike before they strike you, but strike discreetly."

You have to strike far from the ball. The referee, like the TV cameras, keeps his eyes on the ball. In the '70 World Cup, Pelé was marked brutally by the Italian Bertini. Later on he praised him: "Bertini was an artist at committing fouls without being seen. He'd punch me in the ribs or in the stomach, he'd kick me in the ankle.... An artist."

Argentine journalists frequently applaud the tricks of Carlos Bilardo because he knows how to play them carefully and effectively. They say when Bilardo was a player he'd prick his opponents with a pin and look innocent. And when he was coach of the Argentine national team, he managed to send a canteen filled with emetic water to Branco, a thirsty Brazilian player, during the toughest match of the '90 World Cup.

Uruguayan journalists like to call brazen crime a "strong-legged play," and more than one has celebrated the effectiveness of the "softening kick" to intimidate opposing players in international contests. That kick must be given in the first minutes of the match. Later on you run the risk of being sent off. In Uruguayan soccer, violence is the daughter of decadence. Long ago, the "Charrua's claw" was a term for bravery, not for a vicious kick. In the '50 World Cup, during the famous final in Maracaná, Brazil committed twice as many fouls as Uruguay. In the '90 World Cup, when coach Oscar Tabárez managed to get the Uruguayan team to go back to playing cleanly, several local commentators took pleasure in affirming that it didn't achieve much. There are many fans and officials who prefer winning without honor to losing nobly.

Uruguayan forward "Pepe" Sasía said: "Throw dirt in the eyes of the goalkeeper? The managers don't like it when you get caught."

Argentine fans heap praise on the goal Maradona scored with his hand in the '86 World Cup, *because the referee didn't see it.* In the qualifiers for the '90 World Cup, Chile's keeper Roberto Rojas pretended to be wounded by cutting himself on the forehead, but he got caught. The fans, who adored Rojas and called him the "Condor," suddenly turned him into the villain of the picture *because his trick didn't work.*

In professional soccer, like in everything else, the crime doesn't matter as long as the alibi is good. "Culture" means cultivation. What does the culture of power cultivate in us? What could be the sad harvests of a power that offers impunity to the crimes of the military and the graft of politicans and converts them into laudable feats?

The writer Albert Camus, who once was a goalkeeper in Algeria, was not referring to professional soccer when he said: "Everything I know about morals, I owe to soccer."

indigestion

IN 1989 in Buenos Aires, a match between Argentinos Juniors and Racing ended in a draw. The rules called for a penalty shoot-out.

The crowd was on its feet, biting its nails, for the first shots at twelve paces. The fans cheered a goal by Racing. Then came a goal by Argentinos Juniors and the fans from the other side cheered. There was an ovation when the Racing keeper leapt against one post and sent the ball awry. Another ovation praised the Argentinos keeper who did not allow himself to be seduced by the expression on the striker's face and waited for the ball in the center of the goal.

When the tenth penalty was kicked, there was another round of applause. A few fans left the stadium after the twentieth goal. When the thirtieth penalty came around, the few who remained responded with yawns. Kicks came and went and the match remained tied.

After forty-four penalty kicks, the game ended. It was a world record for penalties. In the stadium no one was left to celebrate, and no one even knew which side won.

the 1990 world cup

NELSON MANDELA was free, after spending twenty-seven years in prison for being black and proud in South Africa. In Colombia, the left's presidential candidate Bernardo Jaramillo lay dying from an assassin's bullet, and from a helicopter the police were shooting drug-trafficker Rodríguez Gacha, one of the ten richest men in the world. Chile's badly wounded democracy was recuperating, but General Pinochet, at the head of the military, continued to keep an eye on the politicians and keep them reined in. Fujimori, riding a tractor, beat Vargas Llosa in the Peruvian elections. In Nicaragua, the Sandinistas lost the elections, defeated by the exhaustion wrought by ten years of war against invaders armed and trained by the United

States, while the United States began a new occupation of Panama following the success of their twenty-first invasion of that country.

In Poland, labor leader Lech Walesa, a man of daily mass, was leaving jail and entering the government. In Moscow a crowd was lining up at the doors of McDonald's. The Berlin Wall was being sold off in pieces, as the unification of the two Germanys and the disintegration of Yugoslavia began. A popular insurrection was putting an end to the Ceaucescu regime in Rumania, and the veteran dictator, who liked to call himself the "Blue Danube of Socialism," was being executed. In all Eastern Europe, old bureaucrats were turning into new entrepreneurs and cranes were dragging off statues of Marx, who had no way of saying, "I'm innocent." Well-informed sources in Miami announced the imminent fall of Fidel Castro, it was only a matter of hours. Up in heaven, terrestrial machines were visiting Venus and spying on its secrets, while here on earth, in Italy, the fourteenth World Cup was getting underway.

Fourteen teams from Europe and six from the Americas took part, plus Egypt, South Korea, United Arab Emirates and Cameroon, who astonished the world by defeating the Argentine side in the first match and playing head to head with England. Milla, a forty-year-old veteran, was first drum in this African orchestra.

Maradona, with one foot swelled up like a pumpkin, did the best he could to lead his team. You could barely hear the tango. After losing to Cameroon, Argentina drew with

Rumania and Italy and was about to lose to Brazil. The Brazilians dominated the entire game, until Maradona, playing on one leg, evaded three markers at midfield and set up Caniggia, who scored before you could even exhale.

Argentina faced Germany in the final, just as in the previous Cup, but this time Germany won 1-0 thanks to an invisible foul and Beckenbauer's wise coaching.

Italy took third place, England fourth. Schillaci of Italy led the list of scorers with six, followed by Skuharavy of Czechoslovakia with five. This championship, boring soccer without audacity or beauty, had the lowest average scores in World Cup history.

goal by rincón

IT WAS at the 1990 World Cup. Colombia played better than Germany, but was losing the match 1-0.

Then, in the final minute, the ball reached midfield in search of a head with an electrified afro: Valderrama got the ball from behind, he turned, shook off three Germans he had no need of and passed to Rincón. The ball travelled from Rincón to Valderrama, Valderrama to Rincón, yours and mine, mine and yours, touch after touch, until Rincón loped forward several paces like a giraffe and faced Illgner, the

German keeper, alone. Illgner covered the goal completely. So Rincón didn't kick the ball, he caressed her. And she slid softly between the goalkeeper's legs and scored.

hugo sánchez

AS 1992 unfolded, Yugoslavia fell to pieces. War taught brothers to hate each other, and to kill and rape without remorse.

Two Mexican journalists, Epi Ibarra and Hernán Vera, wanted to go to Sarajevo. Bombarded, under siege, Sarajevo was off limits to the foreign press, and audacity had already cost more than one reporter his life.

Chaos reigned on all approaches to the city. Everyone against everyone else—no one was sure who was who, or who they were fighting in that bedlam of trenches, smoking ruins and unburied bodies. Map in hand, Epi and Hernán made their way through the thunder of artillery-fire and machine-gun blasts, until on the banks of the Drina River they suddenly came face-to-face with a large group of soldiers, who threw them to the ground and took aim at their chests. The officer bellowed who knows what and the reporters mumbled back who knows what else, but when the officer drew his finger across his throat and the rifles went click, they understood that there was nothing left to do but say goodbye and pray, just in case there is a Heaven.

Then it occurred to the condemned men to show their passports. The officer's face lit up. "Mexico!" he screamed. "Hugo Sánchez!"

And he dropped his weapon and hugged them.

Hugo Sánchez, the Mexican key to impossible locks, became world famous thanks to television, which showcased the art of his goals and the handsprings he turned to celebrate them. In the 1989-1990 season, wearing the uniform of Real Madrid, he burst the nets thirty-eight times and became the leading foreign scorer in the entire history of Spanish soccer.

the cicada and the ant

IN 1992 the singing cicada defeated the worker ant 2-0.

Germany and Denmark faced each other in the final of the European Championship. The German players were raised on fasting, abstinence and hard work, the Danes on beer, women and naps in the sun. Denmark had lost out in the qualifiers and the players were on vacation when war intervened and they were called urgently to take Yugoslavia's place in the tournament. They had no time for training nor any interest in it, and had to make do without Michael Laudrup, a brilliant, happy and sure-footed player who had just won the European Cup wearing a Barcelona shirt. The German team, on the other hand, came to the final with Matthaus, Klinsmann and all its stars. Germany, who ought to have won, was defeated by Denmark, who had nothing to prove and played as if the field were a continuation of the beach.

gullit

IN 1993 the tide of racism was rising. Its stench, like a recurring nightmare, already hung over Europe; several crimes were committed and laws against ex-colonial immigrants were passed. Many young whites, unable to find work, tried to pin the blame on people with dark skin.

That year a team from France won the European Cup for the first time. The winning goal was the work of Basile Boli, an African from the Ivory Coast, who headed in a corner kicked by another African, Abedi Pelé, born in Ghana. Meanwhile, not even the blindest proponents of white supremacy could deny that Holland's best players were the veterans Ruud Gullit and Frank Rijkaard, dark-skinned sons of Surinam, or that the African Eusebio had been Portugal's best soccer player ever.

Ruud Gullit, known as "The Black Tulip," had always been

a full-throated opponent of racism. Guitar in hand, he sang at anti-apartheid concerts between games, and in 1987 when he was chosen Europe's most valuable player he dedicated his Golden Boot to Nelson Mandela, who had spent many years in jail for the crime of believing that blacks are human.

One of Gullit's knees was operated on three times. Each time commentators declared he was finished. Out of sheer desire he always came back: "When I can't play I'm like a newborn with nothing to suck."

His nimble scoring legs and his imposing stature crowned by a head of Rasta dredlocks won him a fervent following when he played for the strongest teams in Holland and Italy. But Gullit never got along with coaches or managers because he tended to disobey orders and had the stubborn habit of speaking out against the culture of money that's reducing soccer to just another item on the stock exchange.

parricide

AT THE END of the winter of 1993, Colombia's national team played a World Cup qualifier in Buenos Aires. When the Colombian players took the field, they were greeted with a shower of whistles, boos and insults. When they left, the crowd gave them a standing ovation that echoes to this day.

Argentina lost 5-0. As usual, the goalkeeper carried the cross of the defeat, but this time the visitors' victory was celebrated as never before. Unanimously the Argentine fans cheered the Colombians' incredible style, a feast of legs, a joy for the eyes, an ever-changing dance that invented its own music as the game progressed. The lordly play of "Pibe" Valderrama, a working-class mulatto, was the envy of princes, and the black players were the kings of this carnival. Not a soul could get past Perea or stop "Freight Train" Valencia; not a soul could deal with the tentacles of "Octopus" Asprilla or block the bullets fired by Rincón. Given the color of their skin and the intensity of their joy, those Colombians looked like Brazil in its glory years.

The Colombian press called that massacre a "parricide." Half a century before, the founding fathers of soccer in Bogota, Medellín and Cali were Argentines. But life has its surprises: Pedernera, Di Stéfano, Rossi, Rial, Pontoni and Moreno fathered a child who turned out to be Brazilian.

goal by zico

IT WAS in 1993. In Tokyo, Kashima was playing Tohoku Senai for the Emperor's Cup.

The Brazilian Zico, star of Kashima, scored the winning goal, the most beautiful of his career. The ball reached the center on a cross from the right. Zico, who was in the semi-circle, leapt forward. But he jumped too soon: when he realized the ball was behind him, he turned a somersault in mid air and with his face to the ground he drove it in with his heel. *wow* It was a backwards overhead volley.

"Tell me about that goal," pleaded the blind.

a sport of evasion

WHEN SPAIN was still suffering under the dictatorship of Franco, Real Madrid president Santiago Bernabéu set out a definition of the club's mission: "We are serving the nation. What we want is to make people happy."

And his colleague from Atlético de Madrid, Vicente Calderón, also praised the sport's virtues as a collective valium: "Soccer keeps people from thinking about more dangerous things."

In 1993 and 1994 the directors of several soccer teams around the world were charged and prosecuted for swindles of various sorts. Evidently soccer is useful not only for hiding social tensions and evading social conflict, but for hiding assets and evading taxes.

The days are long gone when the most important clubs in the world belonged to the fans and the players. In those remote times, the club president went around with a bucket of lime and a brush to paint the lines on the field, and as for directors, their most extravagant act was footing the bill for a celebratory feast in the neighborhood pub. Today clubs are corporations who move fortunes to hire players and sell spectacles, and they've grown quite accustomed to tricking the state, fooling the public and violating labor rights and every other right. They are also used to impunity. There is no multinational corporation that enjoys greater impunity than FIFA, the association of professional clubs. FIFA has its own justice system. As in *Alice in Wonderland*, FIFA's unjust justice sentences first and tries later, when there will be plenty of time.

Professional soccer operates at the margins of the law, in a sacred territory where it can dictate its own laws and ignore all others. But why should the law operate at the margins of soccer? Judges rarely dare to red-card the big clubs for cooking the books to score illegal goals on the public treasury and leave the rules of clean play sprawled on the ground. The fact is judges know they risk a sharp whistle if they use an iron hand. Professional soccer is untouchable because it is popular. "The directors steal for us," say the fans, and they believe it.

Some judges are prepared to defy the tradition of impunity, and recent scandals have at least shone some light on the financial acrobatics and shell games that some of the richest clubs in the world play as a matter of course.

When the president of the Italian club Perugia was accused of buying referees in 1993, he counterattacked by claiming, "Eighty percent of soccer is corrupt." ⅃⅃⅃

Experts agree he was being generous. Every important club in Italy, from north to south, from Milan and Torino to Naples and Cagliari, is involved in fraud—some more, some less. Their falsified balance sheets hide debts several times the net worth of their capital; their directors maintain slush funds, phantom companies and secret Swiss accounts; instead of taxes and social security they pay hefty bills for services unrendered; and the players tend to pocket a lot less money than the books say they receive, as it gets lost along the way.

The same tricks are common among the most notorious clubs of France. Several directors of Bordeaux were charged with embezzling funds for personal use, and the head honchos of Olympique de Marseille were taken to court for bribing their opponents. Olympique, the most powerful club in France, was knocked down to the second division and lost the titles of champion of France and of Europe when its directors were caught bribing several players from Valenciennes just before a match in 1993. That episode put an end to the sporting career and political ambitions of the businessman Bernard Tapie, who got a year in prison and ended up bankrupt.

At the same time, the Polish champion club Legia lost its title for having "arranged" two games, and Tottenham Hotspur in England revealed that they had been asked to make under-the-table payments to obtain a player from Nottingham Forest. The English club Luton, meanwhile, was being investigated for tax evasion.

Several soccer scandals erupted simultaneously in Brazil. The president of Botafogo charged that the directors of Brazil's professional league had manipulated seven matches in 1993, winning a small fortune in bets. In São Paulo other lawsuits revealed that a local soccer federation boss had grown rich overnight, and when certain phantom accounts were examined it became clear that his sudden fortune did not result from a life devoted to the noble calling of sport. As if that weren't enough, the president of the Brazilian Soccer Confederation, Ricardo Teixeira, was sued by Pelé for taking bribes in the sale of television broadcast rights. In response to Pelé's suit, Havelange named Teixeira, his son-in-law, to the FIFA board.

Nearly two thousand years before all this, the biblical patriarch who wrote the "Acts of the Apostles" told the story of two early Christians, Ananias and his wife Sapphira, who sold a piece of land and lied about the price. When God found out, he killed them on the spot.

If God had time for soccer, how many directors would remain alive?

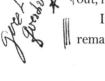

the 1994 world cup

THE MAYAS of Chiapas were up in arms, the real Mexico blowing up in the face of the official Mexico, and subcommander Marcos astonished the world with his words of humor and amour.

Onetti, the novelist of the dark side of the soul, lay dying. World car-racing champion Ayrton Senna, a Brazilian, was decapitated on an unsafe European track. Serbs, Croats and Moslems were killing each other in the pieces that had been Yugoslavia. In Rwanda something similar was happening, but television spoke of tribes, not peoples, and implied that the violence was just a black people's thing.

Torrijos's heirs were winning the Panamanian elections four years after the bloody invasion and useless occupation by the United States. U.S. troops were pulling out of Somalia, where they had fought hunger with bullets. South Africa was voting for Mandela. Communists, rebaptized as socialists, were triumphant in the parliamentary elections in Lithuania, Ukraine, Poland and Hungary, countries that had discovered that capitalism also has certain inconvenient traits. But Moscow's Progress Publishers, which used to publish the works of Marx and Lenin, was now publishing Reader's Digest. Well-informed sources in Miami announced the imminent fall of Fidel Castro, it was only a matter of hours.

Corruption scandals were demolishing Italy's political parties and filling the power vacuum was Berlusconi, the parvenu who ran the dictatorship of television in the name of democratic diversity. Berlusconi crowned his campaign with a slogan stolen from the soccer stadium, while the fifteenth World Cup got underway in the United States, the home of baseball.

The U.S. press gave the matter scant attention and commented: Here soccer is the sport of the future and it always will be. But the stadiums were packed despite a sun that melted stones. To please European television, the big matches were played at noon, as in Mexico at the '86 Cup.

Thirteen teams from Europe, six from the Americas and three from Africa took part, plus South Korea and Saudi Arabia. To discourage ties, three points were given for each win instead of two. And to discourage violence, the referees were much more rigorous than usual, handing out yellow and red cards throughout the tournament. For the first time the referees wore colorful uniforms and for the first time each team was allowed a third substitute to replace an injured goalkeeper.

Maradona played in his final World Cup and it was a party, until he was defeated in the laboratory that tested his urine after the second match. Without him and without the speed-demon Caniggia, Argentina fell apart. Nigeria played the most satisfying soccer of the Cup. Bulgaria, Stoichkov's team, won fourth place after knocking the fearful German squad out of the running. Third place went to Sweden. Italy faced Brazil in the final. It was a boring drawn-out affair that ended scoreless, but between yawns Romario and Baggio offered some lessons in good soccer. In the penalty shoot-out, Brazil won 3-2 and was crowned champion of the world. An amazing story: Brazil is the only country that has qualified for every World Cup, the only country to win four times, the country that has won the most games and the the country that has scored the most goals.

Leading the list of scorers in the '94 Cup were Stoichkov of Bulgaria and Salenko of Russia with six goals, followed by

Brazil's Romario, Italy's Baggio, Sweden's Andersson and Germany's Klinsmann, with five apiece.

romario

FROM WHO-knows-what part of the stratosphere, the tiger appears, mauls and vanishes. The goalkeeper, trapped in his cage, doesn't even have time to blink. Romario fires off one goal after another: half-volley, bicycle, on the fly, banana shot, backheel, toe poke, side tap.

Romario was born poor in a *favela* called Jacarezinho, but even as a child he practiced writing his name to prepare for the many autographs he would sign in his life. He clambered up the ladder to fame without paying the toll of obligatory lies: this very poor man always enjoyed the luxury of doing whatever he wished, a bar-hopping lover of the night who said what he thought without thinking about what he was going to say.

Now he has a collection of Mercedes Benzs and two-hundred-and-fifty pairs of shoes, but his best friends are still that bunch of unpresentable hustlers who, in his childhood, taught him how to make the kill.

baggio

IN RECENT years no one has given Italians better soccer or a better topic of conversation. Roberto Baggio's game is mysterious: his legs have a mind of their own, his foot shoots by itself, his eyes see the goals before they happen.

Baggio is a big horsetail that flicks away opponents as he flows forward in an elegant wave. Opponents harass him, they bite, they punch him hard. Baggio has Buddhist sayings written under his captain's armband. Buddha doesn't ward off the blows, but he does help suffer them. From his infinite serenity, he also helps Baggio discover the silence that lies beyond the din of cheers and whistles.

a few numbers

BETWEEN 1930 and 1994 the Americas won eight world championships and Europe won seven. Brazil won the trophy four times, Argentina twice and Uruguay twice. Italy and Germany were world champions three times apiece; England only won the Cup played on its home turf.

But since Europe's teams formed the overwhelming majority, it had twice as many chances. In fifteen World Cups, European teams had 159 opportunities to win, compared to only seventy-seven opportunities for teams from the Americas. What's more, the overwhelming majority of referees have been European.

Unlike the World Cup, the Inter-Continental Cup has offered the same number of opportunities to the teams of Europe and the Americas. In these tournaments, waged by clubs rather than national teams, squads from the Americas have won twenty times to the Europeans' thirteen.

The case of Great Britain is the most astonishing in this matter of inequality of rights in world soccer championships. The way they explained it to me as a child, God is one but He's three: Father, Son and Holy Ghost. I never could understand it. And I still don't understand why Great Britain is one but she's four: England, Scotland, Northern Ireland and Wales, while Spain and Switzerland, to take two examples, continue to be no more than one despite the diverse nationalities that make them up.

In any case, Europe's traditional control is beginning to break down. Until the '94 World Cup, FIFA accepted one or two token countries from the rest of the world, as if paying a tax to the *mappa mundi*. Starting with the '98 Cup, the number of participating countries will go from twenty-four to thirty-two. Europe will maintain its unjust proportion in relation to the Americas, but it will have to accept greater participation by the countries of black Africa, with its quick happy soccer in full expansion, and also from Arab and Asian countries like the Chinese who pioneered the sport but until now have had to watch from the stands.

the duty of losing

FOR BOLIVIA, qualifying for the '94 World Cup was like reaching the moon. Penned in by geography and mistreated by history, it had attended other World Cups only by invitation and failed to score a single goal.

The work of coach Xabier Azkargorta was paying off, not only in La Paz where you play above the clouds, but at sea level. Bolivia was proving that altitude was not its only great player. They could overcome the hangups that obliged them to lose before the game even began. Bolivia sparkled in the qualifying rounds. Melgar and Baldivieso in the midfield and the forwards Sánchez and above all Etcheverry, known as "El Diablo," were cheered by the most demanding of crowds.

As bad luck would have it, Bolivia had to open the World Cup against all-powerful Germany. A baby finger against Rambo. But no one could have foreseen the outcome: instead of shrinking back into the box, Bolivia went on the attack. They didn't play equal against equal, no—they played as the big guys against the little. Germany, thrown off stride, was in flight and Bolivia was in ecstasy. And that's how it continued, until the moment when Bolivia's star Marco Antonio Etcheverry took the field only to kick Matthaus inexcuseably and get thrown out of the game. Then Bolivia collapsed, wishing they had never sinned against the secret spell cast from the depths of centuries that obliges them to lose.

the sin of losing

SOCCER ELEVATES its divinities and exposes them to the vengeance of the believers. With the ball on his foot and the national colors on his chest, the player who embodies the nation marches off to win glory on far-off battlefields. If he returns defeated, the warrior becomes a fallen angel. At Ezeiza airport in 1958, people threw coins at Argentina's players returning from a poor performance at the World Cup in Sweden. In the '82 Cup, Caszely missed a penalty kick and back in Chile they made his life impossible. Ten years later, several Ethiopian players asked the United Nations for asylum after losing 6-1 to Egypt.

We *are* because we win. If we lose, we no longer exist. Without question, the national uniform has become the clearest symbol of collective identity, not only in poor or small countries whose place on the map depends on soccer. When England lost out in the qualifiers for the '94 World Cup, the front page of the *Daily Mirror* featured a headline in a typesize fit for a catastrophe: "THE END OF THE WORLD."

In soccer, as in everything else, losing is not allowed. In these *fin-de-siècle* days, failure is the only sin that cannot be redeemed. During the '94 World Cup, a handful of fanatics burned down the home of Joseph Bell, the defeated Cameroon goalkeeper, and Colombian player Andrés Escobar was gunned down in Medellín. Escobar had had the bad luck of scoring an own goal, an unforgivable act of treason.

Should we blame soccer? Or should we blame the culture of success and the whole system of power that professional soccer reflects? It is not by nature a violent sport, although at times it becomes a vehicle for letting off steam. It was no coincidence that the murder of Escobar took place in one of the most violent countries on the planet. Violence is not in the genes of these people who love to celebrate and are wild about the joys of music and soccer. Colombians suffer from violence like a disease, but they don't wear it like a birthmark on their foreheads. The machinery of power, on the other hand, is indeed a cause of violence: as in all of Latin America, injustice and humiliation poison people's souls under a system with a tradition of impunity that rewards the unscrupulous, encourages crime and helps to perpetuate it as a national trait.

A few months before the '94 World Cup began, Amnesty International published a report according to which hundreds of Colombians "were executed without due process by the armed forces and their paramilitary allies in 1993. Most of the victims of these extrajudicial executions were people without known political affiliation."

The report of Amnesty International also exposed the role of the Colombian police in "social clean-up" operations, a euphemism for the systematic extermination of homosexuals, prostitutes, drug addicts, beggars, the mentally ill and street children. Society calls them "disposables," human garbage that ought to die.

In this world that punishes failure, they are always the losers.

maradona

HE PLAYED, he won, he peed, he lost. Ephedrine turned up in his urine analysis and Maradona was booted out of the '94 World Cup. Ephedrine, though not considered a stimulant by professional sports in the United States or many other countries, is prohibited in international competitions.

There was stupefaction and scandal, a blast of moral condemnation that left the whole world deaf. But somehow a few voices of support for the fallen idol managed to squeak through—not only in his wounded and dumbfounded Argentina, but in places as far away as Bangladesh, where a sizable demonstration repudiating FIFA and demanding Maradona's return shook the streets. After all, to judge and condemn was easy. It was not so easy to forget that for many years Maradona had committed the sin of being the best, the crime of speaking out about things the powerful wanted kept quiet, and the felony of playing left-handed, which according to the Oxford English Dictionary means not only "of or pertaining to the left hand" but also "sinister or questionable."

Diego Armando Maradona never used stimulants before matches to stretch the limits of his body. It is true that he was into cocaine, but only at sad parties where he wanted to forget or be forgotten because he was cornered by glory and couldn't live without the fame that wouldn't allow him to live. He played better than anyone else in spite of the cocaine, not because of it.

He was overwhelmed by the weight of his own shadow. From that day long ago when fans first chanted his name, his spinal column caused him grief. Maradona carried a burden named Maradona that bent his back out of shape. The body as metaphor: his legs ached, he couldn't sleep without pills. It didn't take him long to realize it was impossible to live with the responsibility of being a god on the field, but from the beginning he knew that stopping was out of the question. "I need them to need me," he confessed, after many years of living under the tyrannical halo of superhuman performance, swollen with cortisone and analgesics and praise, harassed by the demands of his devotees and by the hatred of those he offended.

The pleasure of knocking idols down is directly proportional to the pleasure of erecting them. In Spain, when Goicoechea hit him from behind—even though he didn't have the ball—and sidelined him for several months, some fanatics carried the author of this premeditated homicide on their shoulders. And all over the world plenty of people were ready to celebrate the fall of that arrogant interloper, that parvenu fugitive from hunger, the greaser who had the insolent audacity to swagger and boast.

Later on, in Naples, Maradona was Santa Maradonna, and the patron saint San Gennaro became San Gennarmando. In the streets they sold pictures of this divinity in shorts illuminated by the halo of the Virgin or wrapped in the sacred mantle of the saint who bleeds every six months. And they even sold coffins for the clubs of northern Italy and bottles filled with the tears of Silvio Berlusconi. Kids and dogs wore Maradona wigs. Somebody placed a ball under the foot of the statue of Dante, and in the famous fountain Triton wore the blue shirt of Naples. It had been more than half a century since this city, condemned to suffer the furies of Vesuvius and eternal defeat on the soccer field, had last won a championship, and thanks to Maradona the dark south finally managed to humiliate the white north that scorned it. In the stadiums of Italy and all Europe, Naples kept on winning, cup after cup, and each goal constituted a desecration of the established order and a revenge against history. In Milan they hated the man responsible for this affront by the uppity poor: they called him "ham with curls." And not only in Milan: at the 1990 World Cup most of the spectators punished Maradona with furious whistles every time he touched the ball, and celebrated Argentina's defeat by Germany as a victory for Italy.

When Maradona said he wanted to leave Naples, people tossed wax dolls stuck with pins through his window. Prisoner of the city that adored him, and of the Camorra, the Mafia that owns it, he was playing against his heart, against his feet. That's when the cocaine scandal erupted, and Maradona suddenly became Maracoca, a delinquent who had fooled people into thinking he was a hero.

Later on, in Buenos Aires, the media gave a further twist to the knife: live coverage of his arrest, as if it were a match, to the delight of those who love the spectacle of a king disrobed and carted off by the police.

"He's sick," they said. They said: "He's done for." The Messiah who came to redeem southern Italians from their eternal damnation was also the avenger of Argentina's defeat in the Falklands War by means of one sneaky goal and another fabulous one which left the English spinning like tops for several years. But when he fell, the Golden Boy was nothing but a numb-nosed whoring phony. Maradona had betrayed the children who adored him and brought dishonor on the sport. They gave him up for dead.

But the body sat up. Once he had served his cocaine sentence, Maradona became the fireman of the Argentine team which was burning up its last chances to reach the '94 World Cup. Thanks to Maradona, they made it. And at the Cup once again, as in the old days, Maradona was the best of the best until the ephedrine scandal.

The machinery of power had sworn to get him. He spoke truth to power and you pay a price for that, a price paid in cash with no discount. And Maradona gave them the excuse, with his suicidal tendency to serve himself up on a platter to his enemies and that childish irresponsibility that makes him step in every trap laid in his path.

The same reporters who harass him with their microphones reproach him for his arrogance and his tantrums, and accuse him of talking too much. They aren't wrong, but that's not what they can't forgive him for: what they really don't like are the things he sometimes says. This hot-tempered little wiseacre has the habit of throwing uppercuts. In '86 and '94, in Mexico and the United States, he complained about the omnipotent dictatorship of television which forced the players to work themselves to the bone at noon, roasting under the sun. And on a thousand and one other occasions, through the ups and downs of his career, Maradona said things that stirred up the hornets' nest. He wasn't the only disobedient player, but his was the voice that made the most offensive questions ring out loud and clear. Why aren't the international standards for labor rights applied to soccer? If it's usual for performers to know how much money their shows bring in, why can't the players have access to the books of the opulent multinational of soccer? Havelange, busy with other duties, kept his mouth shut, while Joseph Blatter, a FIFA bureaucrat who never once kicked a ball but goes about in a twenty-five-foot limousine driven by a black chauffeur, had but one comment: "The last star from Argentina was Di Stéfano."

When Maradona was finally thrown out of the '94 World Cup, soccer lost its most strident rebel. And also a fantastic player. Maradona is uncontrollable when he speaks, but much more so when he plays: no one can predict the devilish tricks this inventor of surprises will dream up for the simple joy of throwing the computers off track, tricks he never repeats. He's not quick, more like a short-legged bull, but he carries the ball sewn to his foot and he's got eyes all over his body. His acrobatics light up the field. He can win a match with a thundering blast when his back is to the goal, or with an impossible pass from far off when he's corralled by thousands of enemy legs. And no one can stop him when he decides to dribble upfield.

In the frigid soccer of the end of this century, which detests defeat and forbids all fun, that man was one of the few who proved that fantasy can be efficient.

they don't count for beans

AT THE END of 1994, Maradona, Stoichkov, Bebeto, Francescoli, Laudrup, Zamorano, Hugo Sánchez and other players started organizing an international soccer players union.

The stars of the show have been blindingly absent from the power structures where decisions are made. They don't have the right to say "boo" in the management of local soccer, nor can they enjoy the luxury of being heard in the heights of FIFA where the global pie is divvied up.

Who are the players? Monkeys in a circus? They may dress in silk, but aren't they still monkeys? They are never consulted when it comes to deciding when, where and how they play. The international bureaucracy changes rules at its whim, the players have no say. They can't even find out how much money their legs produce, or where those fugitive fortunes end up.

After many years of strikes and demonstrations by local unions, players have won better contracts, but the merchants of soccer continue treating them as if they were machines to be bought, sold and loaned: "Maradona is an investment," said the president of Naples.

Now European clubs, as well as a few Latin American ones, have psychologists on staff, like in factories. The directors don't pay them to help troubled souls, but to oil the machinery and increase output. Athletic output? Labor output, though in this case the hired hands are really hired feet. The fact is that professional players offer their labor power to the factories of spectacle in exchange for a wage. The price depends on performance, and the more they get paid the more they are expected to produce. Trained to win or to win, squeezed to the last calorie, they're treated worse than racehorses. Racehorses? Paul Gascoigne likes to compare himself to a factory-raised chicken: controlled movements, rigid rules, set behaviors that must always be repeated.

Stars can earn top salaries while their fleeting splendor lasts. Clubs pay them much more now than twenty or thirty years ago, and they can sell their names and faces for advertising. But the glories of soccer idols aren't rewarded with the fabled treasure people imagine. *Forbes* magazine published a list of the forty top-earning athletes in the world in 1994. Among them was only one soccer player, the Italian Roberto Baggio, and he fell near the bottom of the list.

What about the thousands upon thousands of players who are not stars? The ones who don't enter the kingdom of fame, who get stuck going round and round in the revolving door? Of every ten professional soccer players in Argentina, only three manage to make a living from it. The salaries are not great, especially considering the short duration of an active player's career: cannibalistic industrial civilization devours them in a flash.

an export industry

HERE IS the itinerary of a player from the southern reaches of the globe who has good legs and good luck. From his home town he moves to a provincial city, then from the provincial city to a small club in the country's capital. The small club has no choice but to sell him to a large one; the large club, suffocated by debt, sells him to an even larger club in a larger country. And the player crowns his career in Europe.

All along this chain, the clubs, contractors and intermediaries end up with the lion's share of the money. Each link confirms and perpetuates the inequality among the parties, from the hopeless plight of neighborhood clubs in poor countries to the omnipotence of the corporations that run European leagues.

In Uruguay, for example, soccer is an export industry that scorns the domestic market. The continuous outflux of good players means mediocre professional leagues and ever fewer, ever less fervent fans. People desert the stadiums to watch foreign matches on television. When the world championships come around, our players come from the four corners of the earth, meet on the plane, play together for a short while, and bid each other goodbye without ever having the time to gel into a real team, eleven heads, twenty-two legs, a single heart.

When Brazil won its fourth World Cup, only a few of the celebrating journalists managed to hide their nostalgia for the marvels of days past. The team of Romario and Bebeto played an efficient game, but it was stingy on poetry: a soccer much less Brazilian than the hypnotic play of Garrincha, Didí, Pelé and their teammates in '58, '62 and '70. More than one reporter noted the shortage of talent, and several commentators pointed to the style of play imposed by the coach, successful but lacking in magic: Brazil sold its soul to modern soccer. But there was another point that went practically unmentioned: the great teams of the past were made up of Brazilians who played in Brazil. On the '94 team, eight of them played in Europe. Romario, the highest-paid Latin American player in the world, was earning more in Spain than all eleven of Brazil's '58 team put together, who were some of the greatest artists in the history of soccer.

The stars of yesteryear were identified with a local club. Pelé was from Santos, Garrincha from Botafogo and Didí as well, despite a fleeting experience overseas, and you couldn't imagine them without those colors or without the yellow of the national team. That's the way it was in Brazil and everywhere else, thanks to loyalty to the uniform or clauses in the contracts of feudal servitude that until recently tied players for life. In France, for example, clubs had property rights over players until they were thirty-four years old: they could go free once they were all washed up. Demanding freedom, France's players joined the demonstrations of May 1968, when Paris barricades shook the world. They were led by Raymond Kopa.

end of the game

THE BALL TURNS, the world turns. People suspect the sun is a burning ball that works all day and spends the night bouncing around the heavens while the moon does its shift, though science is somewhat doubtful. There is absolutely no question, however, that the world turns around a spinning ball: the final of the '94 World Cup was watched by over two billion people, the largest crowd ever of the many that have assembled in this planet's history. It is the passion most widely shared: many admirers of the ball play with her on fields and pastures, and many more have box seats in front of the TV and bite their nails as they watch the show performed by twenty-two men in shorts who chase a ball and kick her to prove their love.

At the end of the '94 World Cup every child born in Brazil was named Romario, and the turf of the stadium in Los Angeles was sold off like pizza, at twenty dollars a slice. A bit of insanity worthy of a better cause? A primitive and vulgar business? A bag of tricks manipulated by the owners? I'm one of those who believes that soccer might be all that, but it is also much more: a feast for the eyes that watch it and a joy for the body that plays it. A reporter once asked the German theologian Dorothee Sölle: "How would you explain to a child what happiness is?"

"I wouldn't explain it," she answered. "I'd toss him a ball and let him play."

Professional soccer does everything to castrate that energy of happiness, but it survives in spite of all the spites.

And maybe that's why soccer never stops being astonishing. As my friend Angel Ruocco says, that's the best thing about it—its stubborn capacity for surprise. The more the technocrats program it down to the smallest detail, the more the powerful manipulate it, soccer continues to be the art of the unforeseeable. When you least expect it, the impossible occurs, the dwarf teaches the giant a lesson, and a scraggy, bow-legged black man makes an athlete sculpted in Greece look ridiculous.

An astonishing void: official history ignores soccer. Contemporary history texts fail to mention it, even in passing, in countries where it has been and continues to be a primordial symbol of collective identity. I play therefore I am: a style of play is a way of being that reveals the unique profile of each community and affirms its right to be different. Tell me how you play and I'll tell you who you are. For many years soccer has been played in different styles, expressions of the personality of each people, and the preservation of that diversity is more necessary today than ever before. These are days of obligatory uniformity, in soccer and everything else. Never has the world been so unequal in the opportunities it offers and so equalizing in the habits it imposes: in this end-of-century world, whoever doesn't die of hunger dies of boredom.

For years I have felt challenged by the memory and reality of soccer, and I've tried to write something that was worthy of this great pagan mass able to speak such different languages and unleash such universal passion. By writing, I was going to do with my hands what I never could accomplish with my feet: irredeemable klutz, disgrace of the playing fields, I had no choice but to ask of words what the ball I so desired denied me.

From that challenge, and from that need for expiation, this book was born. Homage to soccer, celebration of its lights, denunciation of its shadows. I don't know if it has turned out the way soccer would have liked, but I know it grew within me and has reached the final page, and now that it is born it is yours. And I feel that irreparable melancholy we all feel after making love and at the end of the game.

Montevideo, summer 1995.

epilogue to the 1999 edition

the 1998 world cup

INDIA AND PAKISTAN fulfilled the dream of having their own bombs, and waltzed in through the front door of the exclusive nuclear club of the great powers. Asian stock markets lay prostrate, as did the long dictatorship of Suharto in

Indonesia, emptied of power even while his pockets remained heavy with the sixteen billion dollars power had placed there. The world lost Frank Sinatra, known as the Voice. Eleven European countries agreed to launch a single currency, known as the Euro. Well-informed sources in Miami announced the imminent fall of Fidel Castro, it was only a matter of hours.

João Havelange abdicated the throne and installed in his place the dauphin Joseph Blatter, senior courtesan in the kingdom of world soccer. General Videla, Argentina's former dictator who twenty years earlier had inaugurated the World Cup alongside Havelange, marched off to jail, while in France a new championship got underway.

Despite serious complications caused by a strike at Air France, thirty-two teams arrived at elegant Saint Denis stadium to take part in the final World Cup of the century: fifteen from Europe, eight from the Americas, five from Africa, two from the Middle East, and two from Asia.

Clamors at a victory party, murmurs at a wake: a month of combat in packed stadiums left France, the host, and Brazil, the favorite, waiting to cross swords in the final. Brazil lost 3-0. Suker from Croatia led the list of scorers with six, followed by Batistuta from Argentina and Vieri from Italy, with five apiece.

According to a scientific study reported in the London *Daily Telegraph,* during a match soccer fans secrete nearly as much testosterone as the players. But multinational companies also work up such a lather that you would think they were on the field. Brazil did not become a five-time winner,

but Adidas did. Beginning with the '54 Cup, when Adidas
won with Germany, this was the fifth victory of the players
representing the three bars. With France, Adidas raised the
solid gold world trophy once more. And with Zinedine
Zidane, it took the prize for best player. Rival Nike had to set-
tle for second and fourth places, which it won with Brazil and
Holland. And Nike's star, Ronaldo, was ill for the final. A
junior company, Lotto, scored a coup with Croatia, which
had never been to a World Cup and against all odds won
third place.

Afterwards, the grass at Saint Denis was sold off in slices,
just as at the previous Cup in Los Angeles. The author of this
book has no loaves of lawn to sell, but he would like to offer,
free of charge, a few morsels of soccer that also had something to do with this championship.

stars

THE MOST famous soccer players are products who sell products. Back in Pelé's day, players played and that was all, or
nearly all. By Maradona's time, television and advertising
already held sway and things had changed. Maradona
charged a high price and paid one as well. He charged for his
legs—and paid with his soul.

At fourteen, Ronaldo was a poor mulatto from the slums of Rio de Janeiro, with rabbit teeth and the legs of a great striker, who couldn't play for Flamengo because he didn't have the bus fare. At twenty-two, he was making a thousand dollars an hour, even when he was asleep. Overwhelmed by his own popularity and the pressure of money, obliged to always shine and always win, Ronaldo suffered a nervous breakdown with violent convulsions hours before the '98 Cup was decided. They say Nike forced him to take the field in the final against France. He played, but he didn't. And he couldn't demonstrate the virtues of Nike's new line of boots, the R-9, being marketed on his feet.

prices

AT THE END of the century, soccer reporters write less about players' abilities, and more about the prices they command. Club presidents, businessmen, contractors and related fish mongers crowd the soccer columns. Up to a few years ago "pass" referred to the movement of the ball from one player to another. Now it alludes more to the movement of a player from one club to another, or one country to another. What is the return on investment in the stars? Soccer columnists bombard us with the vocabulary of the times: offer, buy-out, option to buy, sale, foreclosure, appreciation, depreciation. During the '98 World Cup, TV screens across the globe were invaded and overwhelmed by collective emotion, the most collective of emotions. But they also became showcases for commercial exhibition. There were ups and downs in leg futures.

foot labor

JOSEPH BLATTER, soccer's new monarch, gave an interview to the Brazilian magazine *Placar* at the end of '95, while he was still Havelange's right-hand man. The journalist asked him about the international players' union being organized.

"FIFA doesn't deal with players," Blatter responded. "Players are employees of the clubs."

While Blatter the bureaucrat offered his disdain, there was good news for the athletes and for all of us who believe in human rights and freedom for labor. In a suit brought by Belgian soccer player Jean-Marc Bosman, Europe's highest judicial authority, the Supreme Court of Luxembourg, ruled that European players should be free at the end of their contracts.

Later on, Brazil's "Pelé Law" weakened the chains of feudal servitude further. But in many countries, players are still treated as assets of the clubs, most of which are companies disguised as non-profits.

Just before the '98 Cup, coach Pacho Maturana offered this opinion: "Nobody thinks about the players' rights." And that continues to be a truth as large as a house and as vast as the world, even though at long last players are winning the right to free agency. The higher a player goes in professional soccer, the greater are his obligations, always more numerous than his rights. He must live by the decisions of others, suffer military discipline, exhausting training and incessant travel, play day after day after day and always be in top form, producing more and more.

When Winston Churchill reached the age of ninety, buoyant as ever, a journalist asked him the secret of his good health. "Sports," Churchill responded. "I never played them."

advertisements

IN TODAY'S world, everything that moves and everything that doesn't carries some sort of commercial message. Every soccer player is a billboard in movement, but FIFA will not allow players to wear signs of solidarity. Such an affront is expressly prohibited. Julio Grondona, chief of Argentine soccer, reminded us all of this in 1997, when a few players tried to express on the field their support for the demands of the country's teachers, who earn salaries of perpetual fasting. Not long before that, FIFA fined the English player Robbie Fowler for the crime of writing on his shirt a slogan in support of striking stevedores.

roots

MANY of soccer's greatest stars suffer racism for being black or mulatto. On the field they find an alternative to the life of crime to which they've been condemned by statistical average, and thus they become symbols of collective hope.

A recent survey in Brazil showed that two out of three professional players never finished primary school. Many of these—half—have black or brown skin. Despite the invasion of the middle class evident lately on the field, Brazilian soccer today is not much different from the days when Pelé was a child and used to steal peanuts in the train station.

africans

NJANKA, the player from Cameroon, took off from the back, left the entire population of Austria in the dust, and scored the prettiest goal of the '98 Cup. But Cameroon itself did not get far.

When Nigeria, with its joyous soccer, defeated the Spanish team, and Spain tied with Paraguay, Spain's President José María Aznar commented, "Even a Nigerian, even a Paraguayan could take your place." Then, when Nigeria was knocked out of the running, an Argentine commentator decreed, "They're all bricklayers, none of them uses his head to think."

FIFA, which gives awards for fair play, didn't play fair with Nigeria. Even though the team had just won the Olympics, they wouldn't let it be seeded at the top of its group.

Black Africa's teams left the World Cup early, but Africa's children or grandchildren continued to shine on the teams of Holland, France, Brazil and others. Some commentators called them darkies. They never called the others whities.

fervor

IN APRIL 1997 the guerrillas occupying the Japanese embassy in the city of Lima were gunned down. When commandos burst in and carried out their spectacular lightning butchery, the guerrillas were playing soccer. Their leader, Néstor Cerpa Cartolini, died wearing the colors of Alianza, the club he loved.

Few things happen in Latin America that do not have some direct or indirect relation with soccer. Whether it's something we celebrate together, or a shipwreck that takes us all down, soccer counts in Latin America, sometimes more than anything else, even if it is ignored by ideologues who love humanity but can't stand people.

latin americans

MEXICO played well in the '98 Cup. Paraguay and Chile were tough bones to chew. Colombia and Jamaica gave it their best. Brazil and Argentina gave it a lot less then their best, hand-cuffed by strategies that were rather chary in joy and fantasy. On the Argentine squad all joy and fantasy fell to Ortega, master of gambols and arabesques but a crummy actor when it comes to rolling on the ground.

dutch

OF THE Latin American teams, to tell the truth, the one I liked best was Holland. The orange offered a feast for the eyes, with good footwork and quick passes, luxuriating in the ball. Their style was due, in large part, to the contribution of players from South America, descendants of slaves, born in Surinam.

There were no blacks among the ten thousand Dutch fans who traveled to France, but there certainly were on the field: Kluivert, Seedorf, Reiziger, Winter, Bogarde, Davids. The engine of the team, Davids plays and makes plays: he gets his goals and gets in trouble, because he will not accept that black players earn less than white ones.

french

THEY were immigrants or the children of immigrants, nearly all of those wearing blue shirts and singing "La Marseillaise" before each match. Thuram—elevated to the category of national hero for his two magnificent goals—and Henry, Desailly, Viera and Karembeu were from Africa, the Caribbean islands or New Caledonia. Most of the others came from Basque, Armenian or Argentine families.

Zidane, the one most acclaimed, is the son of Algerians. *Zidane for President* wrote anonymous hands on the Arc de Triomphe the day of the celebration. President? There are many Arabs and children of Arabs in France, but not a single one is a member of parliament, much less a minister.

A poll published during the World Cup found that out of every ten people in France four harbor racial prejudice. Racism's double-speak lets you cheer the heroes and curse the rest. Winning the world trophy was celebrated by a crowd comparable only to the one that overflowed the streets half a century ago, when the German occupation finally ended.

fish

IN 1997 an advertisement on Fox Sports exhorted viewers to watch soccer, "See the big fish gobble up the little." An invitation to boredom. Fortunately, on more than one occasion at the '98 Cup, the little fish ate the big ones, bones and all. That's the bright side we sometimes see in soccer—and in life.

the 2002 world cup

A SEASON OF collapses. A terrorist attack leveled the Twin Towers of New York. President Bush rained missiles down upon Afghanistan and razed the dictatorship of the Taliban, which his father and Reagan had suckled. The war against terrorism gave its blessing to military terror. Israeli tanks were demolishing Gaza and the West Bank, so that the Palestinians could continue to pay for the Holocaust they didn't commit.

Spiderman was toppling box-office records. Well-informed sources in Miami announced the imminent fall of Fidel Castro, it was only a matter of hours. What tumbled was Argentina, the model nation, and its currency, government and everything else went down with it. In Venezuela, a coup d'état overthrew President Chávez. A multitude reimposed the deposed, but Venezuelan television, a champion of freedom of information, failed to report this unpleasant fact.

Shattered by its own swindles, the corporate giant Enron, one of the more generous donors to the campaigns of Bush and most US senators, came crashing down. And like dominos, the stock of other sacred monsters tumbled soon thereafter: WorldCom, Xerox, Vivendi, Merck—all because of some small billion-dollar accounting errors. FIFA's largest business partners, ISL and Kirch, also went belly up, but their outrageous bankruptcies failed to keep Joseph Blatter from being installed, by a landslide, on the throne of world soccer. Find someone worse and you'll look good: Blatter the untouchable makes Havelange look like a Sister of Charity.

Bertie Felstead tumbled too, done in by death. Felstead, the oldest man in England, was the sole survivor of that extraordinary soccer match between British and German soldiers on Christmas Day, 1915 in no-man's land. Under the magical influence of a ball that appeared from who knows where, the battlefield became a playing field for a short while, until screaming officers managed to remind the soldiers that they were obliged to hate each other.

Thirty-two teams travelled to Japan and Korea to wage the seventeenth World Cup Championship in the shiny new stadiums of twenty cities. The first World Cup of the new millennium was the first Cup to be played in Asia. Pakistani children sewed the high-tech ball for Adidas that started rolling on opening night in the stadium at Seoul: a rubber chamber, surrounded by a cloth net covered with foam, all inside a skin of white polymer decorated with the symbol of fire. A ball to lure fortunes from the grass.

There were two soccer world cups. One had athletes of flesh and blood. The other, held simultaneously, featured robots. The mechanical players, programmed by software engineers, waged RoboCup 2002 in the Japanese port of Fukuoka, across from the Korean shore. What do the businessmen, technocrats, bureaucrats and ideologues of the soccer industry dream about? Theirs is a recurring dream, ever more like reality, in which players imitate robots.

Sad sign of the times: the twenty-first century sanctifies uniformity in the name of efficiency and sacrifices freedom on the altars of success. "You win not because you're good, rather you're good because you win," noted Cornelius Castoriadis some years ago. He wasn't referring to soccer, but he might as well have been. Wasting time is prohibited, so is losing. Reduced to a job, subjected to the laws of profitability, the game is no longer played. Like everything else, professional soccer seems to be run by the almighty, even if nonexistent, UEB (Union of the Enemies of Beauty).

Obedience, speed, strength and none of those fancy turns: this is the mold into which globalization pours the game. Soccer gets mass-produced, and it comes out colder than a freezer and as merciless as a meat-grinder. It's a soccer for robots. Such boredom supposedly means progress, but historian Arnold Toynbee had already seen enough of that when he wrote, "Civilizations in decline are consistently characterized by a tendency toward standardization and uniformity."

Back to the flesh and blood Cup. In the opening match, more than one quarter of humanity witnessed the first surprise on television.

France, winner of the previous championship, got beaten by Senegal, one of its former colonies and a first-time participant in the World Cup. Against all predictions, France was sidelined in the first round without scoring a single goal. Argentina, the other great favorite, also fell in the first exchange. And then Italy and Spain were sent packing after suffering armed assaults at the hands of the referees. All these powerful teams were done in by twin brothers: the imperative of winning and the terror of losing. The greatest stars of world soccer came to the Cup overwhelmed by the weight of fame and responsibility, and exhausted from the ferocious pace demanded by the clubs for whom they play.

With no World Cup history, no stars, no obligation to win or trepidation about losing, Senegal played in a state of grace and was the revelation of the championship. China, Ecuador and Slovenia also faced a baptism by fire, but were sidelined in the first round. Senegal made it to the quarter-finals undefeated, and no further, but their perpetual dance-steps brought home a simple truth that tends to escape the scientists of the ball: soccer is a game, and those who really play it feel happy and make us happy too. The goal I liked best in the entire tournament was scored by Senegal, back-heel by Thiaw, deft shot by Camara. Another Senegalese, Diouf, dribbled the ball an average of eight times per match, in a championship where that pleasure of the eyes seemed prohibited.

The other surprise was Turkey. Nobody could believe it. They'd been absent from the Cup for half a century. In their first match, against Brazil, the Turkish side was high-handedly cheated by the referee; but they kept flying and ended up winning third place. Their fervor and quality play rendered the experts who had scorned them speechless.

Nearly all the rest was one long yawn. Fortunately, in its final match-ups Brazil remembered that it was Brazil. The team finally let go and played like Brazilians, slipping out of the cage of efficient mediocrity in which the coach, Scolari, had locked them up. Then their four R's, Rivaldo, Ronaldo, Ronaldinho Gaúcho and Roberto Carlos, shone brilliantly and Brazil, at last, turned into a fiesta.

And they were champions. Just before the final, a hundred and seventy million Brazilians stuck pins in German sausages, and Germany succumbed 2-0. It was Brazil's seventh victory in seven matches. The two countries had been finalists many times, but never before had they faced each other in the World Cup. Turkey took third place, South Korea fourth. Translated into market terms, Nike took first and fourth, while Adidas came in second and third.

The Brazilian Ronaldo, recovered after a long injury, led the list of scorers with eight, followed by his compatriot Rivaldo with five, then the Dane Tomasson and the Italian Vieri with four goals apiece. Sukur of Turkey scored the fastest goal in World Cup history, eleven seconds after the match began.

For the very first time, a goalkeeper, the German Oliver Khan, was chosen as best player of the tournament. Such was the terror he inspired that his opponents thought he was a son of that other Khan, Ghengis. But he wasn't.

the sources

Aguirre, José Fernando, *Ricardo Zamora* (Barcelona: Clíper, 1958).

Alcântara, Eurípedes, "A eficiencia da retranca," and other articles by Marcos Sá Corrêa, Maurício Cardoso and Roberto Pompeu de Toledo, special edition of *Veja* (São Paulo), July 18, 1994.

Altafini, José, *I magnifici 50 del calcio mondiale* (Milan: Sterling & Kupfer, 1985).

Anuario mundial de football profesional, vol. 1, no.1, June 1934 (Buenos Aires).

Archetti, Eduardo P., "Estilo y virtudes masculinas," in *El Gráfico: la creación del imaginario del fútbol argentino* (Oslo: University of Oslo, Department of Social Anthropology).

Arcucci, Daniel, "Mágicos templos del fútbol," *El Gráfico*, March 20, 1991 (Buenos Aires).

Arias, Eduardo, *et al.*, *Colombia gol. De pedernera a Maturana. Grandes momentos del fútbol* (Bogota: Cerec, 1991).

Asociación del Fútbol Argentino, *Cien años con el fútbol* (Buenos Aires: Zago, 1993).

Associazione Italiana Arbitri, *75 anni di storia* (Milan: Vallardi, 1987).

Barba, Alejandro, *Foot Ball, Base Ball y Lawn Tennis* (Barcelona: Soler, n/d).

Bartissol, Charles y Christophe, *Les racines du football français* (Paris: Pac, 1983).

Bayer, Osvaldo, *Fútbol argentino* (Buenos Aires: Sudamericana, 1990).

Benedetti, Mario, "Puntero izquierdo," in the anthology *Hinchas y goles. El fútbol como personaje* (Buenos Aires: Desde la gente, 1994).

Blanco, Eduardo, "El negocio del fútbol," *La Maga*, December 7, 1994 (Buenos Aires).

Boix, Jaume and Arcadio Espada, *El deporte del poder* (Madrid: Temas de Hoy, 1991).

Boli, Basile, *Black Boli* (Paris: Grasset, 1994).

Brie, Christian de, "Il calcio francese sotto i piedi dei mercanti," in the Italian edition of *Le Monde Diplomatique*, June 1994, published by Il Manifesto (Rome).

Bufford, Bill, *Among the Thugs: The Experience, and the Seduction, of Crowd Violence* (New York: Norton, 1992).

Camus, Albert, testimony published in Eduardo Galeano's anthology *Su Majestad el fútbol* (Montevideo: Arca, 1994).

———, *Le premier homme* (Paris: Gallimard, 1994).

Cappa, Angel, "Fútbol, un animal de dos patas," *Disenso*, no. 7, Las Palmas de Gran Canaria.

Carías, Marco Virgilio with Daniel Slutzky, *La guerra inútil. Análisis socio-económico del conflicto entre Honduras y El Salvador* (San Jose, Costa Rica: EDUCA, 1971).

Cepeda Samudio, Alvaro, "Garrincha," in *Alrededor del fútbol* (Medellin: University of Antioq uia, 1994).

Cerretti, Franco, *Storia illustrata dei Mondiali di Calcio* (Rome: Anthropos, 1986).

Comisión de asuntos históricos, *La historia de Vélez Sarsfield* (1910/1980) (Buenos Aires, 1980).

Coutinho, Edilberto, *Maracaná, adeus* (Havana: Casa de las Américas, 1980).

Decaux, Sergio, *Peñarol campión del mundo* (Montevideo: Colección "100 años de fútbol," no. 21, 1970).

Délano, Poli, *Hinchas y goles* (antología) (Buenos Aires: Desde la gente, 1994).

Duarte, Orlando, *Todas las Copas del Mundo* (Madrid: McGraw-Hill, 1993).

Dujovne Ortiz, Alicia, *Maradona sono io. Un viaggio alla scoperta di una iden-titá* (Naples: Edizioni Scientifiche Italiane, 1992).

Dunning, Eric, et al., *The Roots of Football Hooliganism* (London/New York: Routledge and Kegan Paul, 1988).

El Gráfico (Buenos Aires), November 8, 1994, "Discurso de João Havelange ante la cámara de Comercio Brasil-USA en Nueva York, el 27 de octubre de 1994."

Escande, Enrique, Nolo. *El fútbol de la cabeza a los pies* (Buenos Aires: Ukamar, 1992).

Faria, Octavio de, et al., *O ôlho na bola* (Rio de Janiero: Gol, 1968).

Felice, Gianni de, "Il giallo della Fifa," *Guerin Sportivo*, January 25, 1995.

Fernández, José Ramón, *El fútbol mexicano: ¿un juego sucio?* (Mexico: Grijalbo, 1994).

Fernández Seguí, J.A., *La preparación física del futbolista europeo* (Madrid: Sanz Martínez, 1977).

Ferreira, Carlos, *A mi juego* . . . (Buenos Aires: La Campana, 1983).

Galiacho, Juan Luis, *Jesús Gil y Gil, el gran comediante* (Madrid: Temas de Hoy, 1993).

Gallardo, César L., *et al., Los maestros* (Montevideo: Colección "100 años de fútbol", no. 12, 1970).

García-Candau, Julián, *El fútbol sin ley* (Madrid: Penthalon, 1981).

——, *Epica y lírica del fútbol* (Madrid: Alianza, 1995).

Geronazzo, Argentino, *Técnica y táctica del fútbol* (Buenos Aires: Lidiun, 1980).

Gispert, Carlos, *et al., Enciclopedia mundial del fútbol*, 6 vols. (Barcelona: Océano, 1982).

Goethals, Raymond, *Le douzième homme* (Paris: Laffont, 1994).

Guevara, Ernesto, *Mi primer gran viaje* (Buenos Aires: Seix Barral, 1994).

Gutiérrez Cortinas, Eduardo, *Los negros en el fútbol uruguayo* (Montevideo: Colección "100 años de fútbol," no. 10, 1970).

Hernández Coronado, Pablo, *Las cosas del fútbol* (Madrid: Plenitud, 1955).

Herrera, Helenio, *Yo* (Barcelona: Planeta, 1962).

Hirschmann, Micael and Kátia Lerner, *Lance de sorte. O futebol e o jogo do bicho na Belle Epoque carioca* (Rio de Janeiro: Diadorim, 1993).

"Historia de la Copa del Mundo" (documentary video and special serial), *El Gráfico* (Buenos Aires), 1994.

"Historia del fútbol," three documentary videos, (Madrid: Transworld International Metrovideo, 1991).

Howe, Don and Brian Scovell, *Manual de fútbol* (Barcelona: Martínez Roca, 1991).

Hübener, Karl Ludolf, *et al., ¿Nunca más campeón mundial? Seminario sobre fútbol, deportes y política en el Uruguay* (Montevideo: Fesur, 1990).

Huerta, Héctor, *Héroes de consumo popular* (Guadalajara: Agata, 1992).

Ichah, Robert, *Platini* (Paris: Inéditions, 1994).

Il Manifesto (Rome), "Lezioni di Storia" (series of four supplements), June/July 1994.

La República (Montevideo), December 1, 1993, "Entrevista con cuatro integrantes de la 'barra brava' del club Nacional."

230 ✦

Lago, Alessandro dal, *Descrizione di una battaglia. I rituali del calcio* (Bologna: Il Mulino, 1990).

——, with Roberto Moscati, *Regalateci un sogno. Miti e realtá del tifo calcistico in Italia* (Milan: Bompiani, 1992).

——, with Pier Aldo Rovatti, *Per gioco. Píccolo manuale dell'esperienza ludica* (Milan: Cortina, 1993).

La Maga (Buenos Aires), "Homenaje al fútbol argentino," special edition, Jan/Feb 1994.

Lazzarini, Marta and Patricia Luppi, "Reportaje a Roberto Perfumo," in *Boletín de temas de psicología social* (Buenos Aires), vol 2, no. 5, September 1991.

Lever, Janet, *La locura por el fútbol* (Mexico: FCE, 1985).

Loedel, Carlos, *Hechos y actores del profesionalismo* (Montevideo: Colección "100 años de fútbol," no. 14, 1970).

Lorente, Rafael, *Di Stéfano cuenta su vida* (Madrid: n/p, 1954).

Lorenzo, Juan Carlos and Jorge Castelli, *El Fútbol en un mundo de cambios* (Buenos Aires: Freeland, 1977).

Lucero, Diego, *La boina fantasma* (Montevideo: Colección "100 años de fútbol," no. 20, 1970).

Marelli, Roberto, *Estudiantes de La Plata, campeón intercontinental* (Buenos Aires: Norte, 1978).

Mário Filho, *O romance do foot-ball* (Rio de Janeiro: Pongetti, 1949).

——, *O negro no futebol brasileiro* (Rio de Janeiro: Civilização Brasileira, 1964).

——, *Histórias do Flamengo* (Rio de Janeiro: Record, 1966).

——, *O sapo de Arubinha* (São Paulo: Companhia das Letras, 1994).

Martín, Carmelo, Valdano. *Sueños de fútbol* (Madrid: El País/Aguilar, 1994).

Maturana, Francisco with José Clopatofsky, *Talla mundial* (Bogota: Intermedio, 1994).

Mercier, Joseph, *Le football* (Paris: Presses Universitaires, 1979).

Meynaud, Jean, *Sport et politique* (Paris: Payot, 1966).

Milá, Mercedes, "La violencia en el fútbol," segment of television programme "Queremos saber," Antena 3 de Televisión (Madrid), January 1993.

Miná, Gianni, "Le vie del calcio targate Berlusconi," *La Repubblica* (Rome), May 6, 1988.

——, "I padroni del calcio. La Federazione s'é fatta holding," *La Repubblica* (Rome), July 19, 1990.

——, with other members of the Committee, "La classe non è acqua" in *Te Diegum* (Milan: Leonardo, 1991).

Morales, Franklin, "Historia de Nacional" and "Historia de Peñarol," supplements to *La Mañana* (Montevideo), 1989.

——, *Fútbol, mito y realidad* (Montevideo: Collección "Nuestra Tierra," no. 22, 1969).

——, *Los albores del fútbol uruguayo* (Montevideo: Colección "100 años de fútbol," no. 1, 1969).

——, *La gloria tan temida* (Montevideo: Colección "100 años de fútbol", no. 2, 1969).

——, *Enviado especial (I)* (Montevideo: Banco de Boston, 1994).

Morris, Desmond, *The Soccer Tribe* (London: Jonathan Cape, 1981).

Moura, Roberto, testimonies of Domingos da Guia and Didí, *Pesquisa de campo*, published by the University of the State of Rio de Janeiro, June 1994.

Mura, Gianni, "Il calcio dei boia," *La Repubblica* (Rome), November 29, 1994.

Nogueira, Armando, *et al.*, *A Copa que ninguém viu e a que não queremos lembrar* (São Paulo: Companhia das Letras, 1994).

Orwell, George, *et al.*, *El fútbol* (Buenos Aires: Jorge Alvarez, 1967).

Ossa, Carlos, *La historia de Colo-Colo* (Santiago, Chile: Plan, 1971).

Panzeri, Dante, *Fútbol, dinámica de lo impensado* (Buenos Aires: Paidós, 1967).

Papa, Antonio and Guido Panico, *Storia sociale del calcio in Italia* (Bologne: Il Mulino, 1993).

Pawson, Tony, *The Goalscorers, From Bloomer to Keegan* (London: Cassell, 1978).

Pedrosa, Milton (ed.), *Gol de letra* (antología) (Rio de Janeiro: Gol, n/d).

Pepe, Osvaldo, *et al.*, *El libro de los Mundiales* (Buenos Aires: Crea, 1978).

Perdigão, Paulo, *Anatomía de uma derrota* (Porto Alegre: L & PM, 1986).

Peucelle, Carlos, *Fútbol todotiempo e historia de "La Máquina"* (Buenos Aires: Axioma, 1975).

Pippo, Antonio, *Obdulio desde el alma* (Montevideo: Fin de Siglo, 1993).

Platini, Michel, with Patrick Mahé, *Ma vie comme un match* (Paris: Laffont, 1987).

Ponte Preta, Stanislaw, *Bola na rede: a batalha do bi* (Rio de Janeiro, Civilização Brasileira, 1993).

Poveda Márquez, Fabio, *El Pibe. De Pescaíto a la gloria* (Bogota: Intermedio, 1994).

Puppo, Julio César, "El Hachero" in *Nueve contra once* (Montevideo: Arca, 1976).

——, *Crónicas de fútbol* (Montevideo: Enciclopedia Uruguaya, 1969).

Rafael, Eduardo, "Memoria: José Manuel Moreno," *El Toque* (Buenos Aires), March 17, 1994.

Ramírez, Miguel Angel, "Los cachirules: la historia detrás de la nota," *Revista Mexicana de Comunicación*, no. 1, Sept/Oct 1988.

——, "Emilio Maurer contra Televisa, una batalla épica en el fútbol local," *La Jornada* (Mexico), December 7-12, 1993.

Reid, Alastair, *Ariel y Calibán* (Bogota: Tercer Mundo, 1994).

Ribeiro, Péris, *Didí, o gênio da folha seca* (Rio de Janeiro: Imago, 1993).

Rocca, Pablo, *Literatura y fútbol en el Uruguay* (1899/1990) (Montevideo: Arca, 1991).

Rodrigues, Nelson, *A sombra das chuteiras imortais* (São Paulo: Companhia das Letras, 1993).

——, *A pátria em chuteiras* (São Paulo: Companhia das Letras, 1994).

——, with Mário Filho, *Fla-Flu* (Rio de Janeiro: Europa, 1987).

Rodríguez Arias, Miguel, "Diego" (documentary video), (Buenos Aires: Las Patas de la Mentira, 1994).

Rodriguez, Nelson, *El fútbol como apostoloado* (Montevideo: Juventus/Colegio de Escribanos, 1995).

Rowles, James, *El conflicto Honduras-El Salvador* (1969) (San José, Costa Rica: EDUCA, 1980).

Ruocco, Angel, "Grandes equipos italianos en zozobra," (ANSA) in El País (Montevideo), January 16, 1994.

Ryswick, Jacques de, *100,000 heures de football* (Paris: La Table Ronde, 1962).

Saldanha, João, *Meus amigos* (Rio de Janeiro: Nova Mitavaí, 1987).

——, *Futebol e outras histórias* (Rio de Janeiro: Record, 1988).

Salvo, Alfredo di, *Amadeo Carrizo* (Buenos Aires: n/p, 1992).

Sanz, Tomás and Roberto Fontanarrosa, *Pequeño diccionario ilustrado del fútbol argentino* (Buenos Aires: Clarín/Aguilar, 1994).

Sasía, José, *Orsai en el paraíso* (Montevideo: La Pluma, 1992).

Scliar, Salomão (ed.), *et al, A história ilustrada do futebol brasileiro*, 4 vols. (São Paulo: Edobras, n/d).

Scopelli, Alejandro, *¡Hola, mister! El fútbol por dentro* (Barcelona: Junventud, 1957).

Scher, Ariel and Héctor Palomino, *Fútbol: pasión de multitudes y de élites* (Buenos Aires: Cisea, 1988).

Schumacher, Harald, *Der anpfiff. Enthüllungen über den deutschen fussball* (Munich: Knaur, 1987).

Seiherheld, Alfredo and Pedro Servín Fabio, *Album fotográfico del fútbol paraguayo* (Asuncion: Editorial Histórica, 1986).

Shakespeare, William, *The Comedy of Errors* (London: Methuen, 1907).

——, *King Lear* (London: Samuel French, 1967).

Shaw, Duncan, *Fútbol y franquismo* (Madrid: Alianza, 1987).

Silva, Thomaz Soares de, *Zizinho. O mestre Ziza* (Rio de Janeiro: Maracaná, 1985).

Simson, Vyv and Andrew Jennings, *Dishonored Games: Corruption, Money and Greed at the Olympics* (New York: Shapolsky, 1992).

Smorto, Giuseppe, "Nazione corrotto, calco infetto," *La Repubblica* (Rome), March 26, 1993.

Sobrequés, Jaume, *Historia del Fútbol Club Barcelona* (Barcelona: Labor, 1994).

Soriano, Osvaldo, *Cuentos de los años felices* (Buenos Aires: Sudamericana, 1994).

Souza, Roberto Pereira de, "O poderoso chefão," *Playboy* (Brazilian edition), May 1994.

Stárosin, Andréi, *Por esas canchas de fútbol* (Moscow: Lenguas Extranjeras, 1959).

Suburú, Nilo J., *Al fútbol se juega así. Catorce verdades universales* (Montevideo: Tauro, 1968).

——, *Primer diccionario del fútbol* (Montevideo: Tauro, 1968).

Teissie, Justin, *Le football* (Paris: Vigot, 1969).

Termes, Josep, *et al, Onze del barça* (Barcelona: Columna, 1994).

The Times (London), "Interview with João Havelange," February 15, 1991.

234

Thibert, Jacques, *La fabuleuse histoire du football* (Paris: Odil, 1974).

Traverso, Jorge, *Primera línea* (Montevideo: Banco de Boston, 1992).

Uriarte, María Teresa, *et al*, *El juego de pelota en Mesoamérica. Raíces y supervivencia* (Mexico: Siglo XXI, 1992).

Valdano, Jorge, "La ocurrencias de Havelange," *El País* (Madrid), May 28, 1990.

Verdú, Vicente, *El fútbol. Mitos, ritos y símbolos* (Madrid: Alianza, 1980).

Vinnai, Gerhard, *El fútbol como ideología* (Mexico: Siglo XXI, 1974).

Volpicelli, Luigi, *Industrialismo y deporte* (Buenos Aires: Paidós, 1967).

Wolstenholme, Kenneth, *Profesionales del fútbol* (Barcelona: Molino, 1969).

Zito Lema, Vicente, *Conversaciones con Enrique Pichon-Rivière* (Buenos Aires: Cinco, 1991).

index

242 🎵